MY
TRANSITION
HOURS

Goodluck
EBELE JONATHAN

My Transition Hours
Copyright © 2018 Goodluck Ebele Jonathan

Ezekiel Books
PO Box 5172
Kingwood, TX 77325

All rights reserved. No part of this book may be reproduced or transmitted in any form or by any means without written permission of the author.

ISBN-13: 978-1-7324922-6-4
Printed in the United States of America

No part of this book may be reproduced or transmitted in any form or by any means, electronic or mechanical—including photocopying, recording, or by any information storage and retrieval system—without permission in writing from the publisher.

Contents

Foreword	*v*
Acknowledgement	*vii*
Prologue	1
Chapter One Reflections	3
Chapter Two My Political Odyssey	11
Chapter Three Politics & Patriotism- The Fuel Subsidy Dilemma	19
Chapter Four The Chibok School Girls Affair	27
Chapter Five Corruption- The Blame Game	37
Chapter Six Power Struggle	51
Chapter Seven Presidential Campaign	57
Chapter Eight Presidential Election	69
Chapter Nine The World Responds	81
Chapter Ten The Change Game	95
Chapter Eleven The Last Days	111
Chapter Twelve The Youth Bulge	123
Chapter Thirteen Private Sector Reform & Africa Renaissance	131
Chapter Fourteen A Strong Democracy	141
Chapter Fifteen Post Presidential Experience	153
Epilogue	169
References	181
Index	187

Foreword

On Thursday May 17, 2018, I was casually reading a paper and a headline caught my attention. The headline read 'My re-election not worth spilling of blood'. These were the words of a Nigerian Governor from the ruling party. Those words made me smile because they show the impact of the non-violent political philosophy my dear friend and brother, Dr. Goodluck Jonathan, has espoused throughout his political career.

"My political ambition is not worth the blood of any citizen"- Goodluck Jonathan. Those immortal words form the basis of the lasting admiration I have for this man of peace and great son of Africa.

So timeless and universal that even his political opponents have imbibed them. That is influence! If every African leader had such an outlook, our continent would have been light years ahead of where it is today.

In Ghana, we give a lot of credence to the words of our great leader and founding father, Kwame Nkrumah, who once said: "Those who would judge us merely by the heights we have achieved would do well to remember the depths from which we started."

Today, Nigeria has a degree of political stability and it is easy to take that for granted. However, I would want to point out that 2015 marked the first time when a Presidential election was held in Nigeria and the results of the poll was not challenged in court.

When you take this into account, you begin to have an understanding of how one man's leadership ended a negative precedent and opened up the vista for a better political future for the Giant of Africa, as Nigeria is often called.

Dr. Jonathan and I share in common the fact that we were thrust into power by the death of our bosses and that we subsequently went on to win elections to the Presidency in our own rights. The similarities continue in that we both focused on deepening democracy in Africa in our post presidential life.

And here again, I must express my gratitude to Dr. Jonathan for the leadership he showed. There was no bitterness in him after he left power. He did not look back. He did not look down. Instead he looked up and after looking up, he faced forward and went on pressing ahead.

That forward movement has resulted in this work of statecraft and statesmanship of which I am privileged to write the foreword. Though there are many themes in this book, My Transition Hours, the theme that most excites me is the one on youth and the next generation.

Very few African leaders have the moral authority to write on this subject as Dr. Jonathan who lifted millions of youths out of poverty through innovative initiatives like the Youths Enterprise With Innovation in Nigeria (YouWIN), adjudged by the World Bank as probably the most successful business growth competition in the world. Dr. Jonathan also has the enviable record of building more schools (165 elementary/high schools and 14 Universities) for the youth of Nigeria, a feat which led to a massive increase in Nigeria's GDP because, as every leader should know, the more you learn, the more you earn.

In one of the speeches he gave after leaving office, I learnt the meaning of the word opportunity. I learnt that there are three of the letter O in the word tomorrow and none in the word yesterday. And this has motivated me to help Africa and its youth prepare for tomorrow.

I endorse this work and recommend it as necessary reading for all who care about leadership in Africa and the achievable great future ahead of the continent's youth.

Indeed, I agree with President Jonathan that we Africans "are all brothers and sisters borne from the womb of one" Africa.

John Dramani Mahama
President, Republic of Ghana
2012-2017

Acknowledgement

No book or work of art, no matter how small or short, bears the mark of only the author. At every stage, from conception to point of sale, there are always other people involved whose inputs are vital to the final outcome. The experience was not different, in the making of this compact and time-specific work, 'My Transition Hours'.

First, I acknowledge God Almighty, the Source of my strength and Saviour, whose grace has always been sufficient for me. I thank my wife, Mrs. Patience Jonathan, my mother, Madam Eunice Ayi Afeni, and other members of my family for their unalloyed support and encouragement in documenting this experience. They are always there for me in good and difficult times.

If I had been as upbeat and enthusiastic as a group of friends, associates and aides with whom I initially shared the idea of this work, a book on my transition hours would have been out soon after I left office. The totality of the events in the build up to the 2015 polls, the Election Day realities, handover procedures as well as activities in the following days and months was an experience I was keen on documenting, to open to Nigerians that often-shut window of intense considerations and calculations that feed into our politics at critical times.

I had considered that such spotlight would further illuminate the path to building a stronger democracy in our nation. Although it was entirely my decision to do this, I will acknowledge that the encouragement and constant reminders from these associates of mine went a long way in facilitating the process of actualizing the bid.

They are indeed many, but let me mention a few of them. I appreciate King Amalate J. Turner, Senator Nenadi Usman, Azibaola Robert, Dr. Azibapu Godbless Eruani, Yinka Odumakin, Lindsay Barret and Ms. Albertine Doibo for their invaluable contributions and diligent review of the draft. I also thank Ms. Angelle Kwemo, Thierry Ngoufan and Ms. Samantha Elphick for the worthy perspectives they offered in the early days of conceiving this idea.

My special thanks go to Reno Omokri, Gloria Dede, my Executive Assistant and Ikechukwu Eze, my Media Aide, for their unyielding support in the course of my piecing together all the loose ends.

Finally, I express my profound gratitude to everyone who had one thing or the other to do with the process of writing this book. I appreciate you all.

Prologue

It was a moment of truth for our Nation. It does not come frequently. I reached for the telephone and placed a call. An inner peace that I had never felt throughout my political sojourn started to descend upon me. I smiled at the thought of what I was about to do as I waited calmly for the person at the other end of my call to answer.

And the voice I was expecting came on, "Hello.........Your Excellency!"

When I said severally that 'my political ambition is not worth the blood of any Nigerian', I really meant it. This phrase instinctively became a creed and my philosophy on power. It became a principle embedded in my core from when I became Governor of Bayelsa State in 2005 and more evidently during my gubernatorial campaign between 2006 and 2007. It has remained with me and has been the bedrock of my political career and the foundation of the celebrated 'phone call' to my opponent in the 2015 general elections.

There is nothing wrong with being ambitious. The human race strives on continuous growth and development. I am ambitious and desired career progression in all the places I worked before going into politics and even in politics I aspired to advance my political career. However, when ambition is unbridled, when it is not restrained, when limits or boundaries are not placed on it, ambition can take a very great toll on its holder and those it is meant to serve in the case of public office.

There is also nothing wrong in seeking power. I have learnt from my political ascendancy in the sixteen years that I served from Deputy Governor to President that power is a shield, for the one who wields it and for the people it serves. I understand that power will protect you and enable you protect your charges. It will provide a shade from the blistering heat of the sun. When it is raining you can use it as an umbrella to protect yourself and the people you are meant to serve. And when you come to a river, you can convert it to a vessel that will help you and those who you lead to cross.

I learnt from history and personal experience that if you use power as a sword, instead of a shield, it will begin to drain the life out of you and cause untold hardship on those you serve. Too often, many people who see power from the sidelines erroneously believe that the man who uses power as a sword is the strong man. But this is not true. Real power is strength under control.

Only a strong man can wield great power over men and restrain himself from using it to his advantage, if doing so will be to the disadvantage of his people. I believe that any leader who insists on exercising most of the powers assigned to him in the constitution will end up being a nuisance to the society and a problem to himself.

It takes conscience to use power as a shield and ego to use power as a sword. Adolf Hitler and Mahatma Gandhi were both intelligent, disciplined and passionate leaders. But the former destroyed himself and his country. Being led by ego, he used power as a sword. The latter built up his nation and secured her independence from Great Britain and his place in history because he was led by conscience and used power as a shield.

A lot has been said and written about my actions and inactions but as the saying goes, unless the lion learns to write, the tale of the hunt will always glorify the hunter.

I must be emphatic that this book is not my biography, as that will come later. This book reveals how I used power as a shield in the service to our nation and God. I have never claimed to be flawless, so bear that in mind as you go through the truth about *My Transition Hours* as I remember them.

Chapter One

REFLECTIONS

"I call on you to join me to work together in harmony and synergy to forge a nation where we understand our differences instead of pretending they do not exist and work towards a perfect union founded on transparency, equity and justice"

Goodluck Ebele Jonathan
SEPTEMBER 15, 2011: DECLARATION OF INTENT FOR THE
2011 PRESIDENTIAL RACE VIA FACEBOOK

The circumstances of my family background, birth and childhood would not have led anyone to believe that I would ever assume office as President of Nigeria. It was completely unimaginable. I was from a poor family and a minority ethnic group in Nigeria.

My humble beginning is already a known story, at least in parts, but I must state that the 'canoe building' part of my family's origin is a clear testament of how indigent we were at that time. I was born on the 20th of November, 1957, the twilight of British colonial rule in Nigeria. My childhood coincided with the foundational years of an independent Nigeria structured by the British colonial powers.

In retrospect, the period of my childhood had an uncanny bearing on my presidency from 2010-2015. This is because the rivalry between our Founding Fathers and the regions they represented led to tensions which eventually led to the civil war in the early years of the newly independent Nigeria. The same unhealthy rivalry existed in Nigeria in 2010 when I took over and ultimately led to the creation of blocs; the Northern Elders Political Leaders Forum (NEPLF) and the Southern Nigeria People's Assembly (SPLA), its equivalent in the South. This led to tensions that manifested themselves in various acts of threats and violence that required tact and discretion to handle.

In spite of the threats and provocations to make the nation 'ungovernable' for me, I had the overwhelming support of Nigerians in the run up to the Presidential election in 2011. I was able to win the election by the grace of God and the love of Nigerians. The election was all but won even before the whistle was blown because of some strong factors. To mention a few, the pressure to preclude me from contesting in 2011 met with solid indignation from majority of Nigerians.

It was seen as a continuation of the spirited attempt to prevent me from accessing my constitutional right as successor to the Presidency after the sad and untimely death of the late President Umaru Musa Yar'Adua in May 2010 simply because, in the view of some people, I was from the wrong part of the country. Having had to deal with these issues between 2010 and 2011, they again reared their ugly heads in the run up to the 2015 elections, but this time disguised as patriotism. Though I was a sitting President in the Nigerian political firmament, I was an outsider that needed to be stopped at all costs.

My party, the Peoples Democratic Party (PDP), presented a front which, in reality was not united, as the party was already imploding along ethnic and religious lines. This time around, there were Governors who were rounding off their eight year tenures and were blinded by ambition.

Some Governors wanted to be Vice President whilst others strived to be President. If I contested, none could realize his ambition. This muffled implosion would fully manifest in the build up to 2015, with each ship-jumper calculating how much he or she would take from the PDP or the most opportune moment to cause maximum damage and based on that, plot their exit. Unfortunately, some of them are facing persecution in the very place they thought they would be greeted with celebration.

As they jumped ship in preparation for the 2015 elections, only very few of this lot, if any at all, bothered about what the PDP did or did not do in terms of delivering on our campaign promises. Their opposition to my re-election was principally driven by personal ambition. They therefore played up the issue of where I come from and the faith I profess to fuel their burning ambitions. My performance mattered quite little, if it mattered at all.

Our message during the campaigns resonated well with the youth and millions of ordinary Nigerians who saw themselves in our mirror. I was not a product of the power blocs that have held sway over Nigeria since 1966, yet here I was, inside the throne room despite human preferences.

Against the run of my popular emergence, it was an irony that a thick wave of arranged criticism targeted my administration even before the government took off in 2011. My leadership was also pointedly attacked in personal terms as never before experienced. The seed of an ostensibly nationwide disdain was being sown laboriously. I knew a campaign season had started as soon as one had finished. There was nothing yet on ground to go by but the opposition was quite adept at manufacturing negative stories.

If constant scrutiny is acceptable as a phenomenon of democracy, constant fabrication of damaging stories is not. Many reasons make the onslaught in this context very suspect, especially as it was being managed by foreign experts mostly from the United States of America.

Throughout my tenure in office as President, there was a constant barrage of what Donald Trump has now termed 'fake news' coming from a well-oiled media propaganda machine. I can say as a matter of fact that there were never any snipers in training or already trained. There were no lists of political enemies to be taken out. There was no missing $49.8 billion and more importantly I can say that even those who made these and other allegations knew they were false. This probably explains why many of these allegations died a natural death even as the echoes of my retreating footsteps still resounded nationally and globally.

The personal insults, unfounded negative accusations and calculated vicious attacks directed at me and my administration during and immediately after, including up to this very moment may be seen for what they are when this book is read.

Most prominent of the insults was when some members of the opposition referred to my Presidency as clueless. The Office of the President of the Federal Republic of Nigeria has enormous human and material resource attached to it. My administration recorded many firsts in terms of appointments and national development. To say the least, my tenure as President saw Nigeria achieve phenomenal economic growth, becoming the largest economy in Africa in 2013.

We were elected twice into the Security Council of the United Nations (UN). Those who are adept at international politics would appreciate the level of diplomacy involved in getting elected in the United Nations Security Council (UNSC), the most powerful organ of the UN. On the five occasions Nigeria was elected to the Security Council since independence in 1960, two of those times were during my administration. Nigeria was elected into the UNSC in the following years; 1966 - 1967; 1978-1979; 1994-1995; 2010-2011 and 2013 -2015. My team and I were certainly not clueless but filled with immense intellectual capacity and one of the best cabinets in the history of Nigeria.

It was also during my administration that for the first time a Nigerian, Akinwumi Adesina, was elected as the President of the African Development Bank, following deft diplomacy and rewarding consultations. Nigeria had pursued this position unsuccessfully in the past and I consider it a blessing and a great honour to have worked with the incredibly great minds who served in my team.

In retrospect, I never intended going into politics at the time I embraced it but I wholeheartedly accepted the challenge as soon as the opportunity came and my family and friends convinced me to participate. If you speak with my mother, you would not need to prompt her too far before she reveals to you her observations of my traits from birth. It should suffice to quote my mother, Madam Eunice Ayi Afeni, on such very personal note;

> *"From conception to birth, my son gave me peace. He was never sick. As a young boy, he never complained about the workload assigned to him. He was always intervening to restore peace whenever there was a problem between his friends and other kids in the village".*

I could easily understand if my dear mother's words are found by some to be fawning adoration, with no correlation to a discourse as serious as national, regional or global leadership. However, I can say with great relief that it speaks to my own reality. My mother endowed my core essence at a very early age and those words might prove very useful in understanding my public personae. Her perspective into my life is unique, coming from a motherly introspection of a tenant in her womb and diner at her bosom.

Suffice to say, these words capture my attitude to life and dictates my initiative or response to every situation I walk into, find myself in or which life throws at me. The pursuit of peace has always been my priority, above all else. I tend to endeavour for peace no matter the price tag attached to it, totally convinced in my being that the option would lead to a better outcome. My mother's words shed light on and give power to comprehending the unrelenting pursuit of peace which burns deep inside of me.

'Depart from evil and do good; Seek peace, and pursue it.'
Psalm 34:14

The above Bible verse summarizes my attitude to peace. It also prepares peace agents for great rigor and acquisition of intelligence. You do not seek that which is readily available and in the open. You seek peace because it is in hiding. You pursue peace because it is always in flight. You therefore need a greater pace than peace in flight. Peace is never in stasis.

In Nigeria, elections are automatically followed up by litigation. By norm, no election was concluded before court pronouncement since losers would always go to court as if it is a compulsory part of the electoral process. In fact, election petition is an integral part of the struggle for power. I personally view it more as a practice that may negatively impact on the growth of our democracy.

The 2015 Presidential election will go down in Nigeria's history as the first time the winner did not face a legal challenge to his victory. Why did I do that? I did that because my ambition is not worth the blood of any Nigerian. My interest was to move the country forward. My personal principles drove me to take the decision and I am a fulfilled man today as a result of putting the interest of my country ahead of my own. The ordinary people would have borne the brunt of my choice to resist and the rest of West Africa would have been flooded by a large proportion of Nigeria's considerable population as refugees.

My term as Nigeria's President terminated on the 29th of May 2015 and I am of unshaken conviction that my last months and moments in office should be documented as they are an integral part of the democratic development of Nigeria and Africa.

This book is a personal account of my stewardship in the heady days in which brinkmanship was the order of the day in Nigeria, thrusting upon us the responsibility to rein in our nation from a needless dangerous precipice by a menacing and rather tragic political mercantilism. For security reasons, certain information cannot be released now.

It details the months and weeks leading up to my unprecedented and unanticipated phone call to Major-General Muhammadu Buhari (rtd) on the 31st of March 2015 to concede the 2015 Presidential election. It captures my return to private life in the days which followed that very deliberate and well thought out concession call. I have also provided a glimpse of my unexpected entry into full-blown politicking that will interest the reader. My first few tepid steps raised many questions in my mind and these questions go back to the issues the man in the streets is grappling with today.

I will touch on the issue of subsidy on petroleum products and the Chibok School girls kidnap by Boko Haram terrorists in 2014. I intend to give the reader a clear chance to comprehend my actions and the projections of my government on these two events of great significance among many. I choose these events among many others which I intend to address in detail in my biography, not only because of the main national arteries they were attached to but also because of their timing. The former came at a fairly early moment of our administration and the latter in the home stretch. They provided ammunition for the opposition's huge propaganda machine which derived some political momentum and I will address them in some detail.

As you read through My Transition Hours, I urge you to ponder on the following; Did I know what I was going to do if I lost the election? Did I believe the electoral process was free and fair? What led to my decision to concede? What goes on in the mind of a President committed to the peace and development of his country?

These concerns and doubts will be addressed as you follow my odyssey as the lead actor in this epic. This personal account of My Transition Hours is for all those who believe in me and my vision for our country; for people of all races, all manner of diversities and particularly for those who seek truth, peace, good democratic processes, freedom and the rights of mankind around the world.

Chapter Two

MY POLITICAL ODYSSEY

"I have come to launch a campaign of ideas, not one of calumny. I have come to preach love, not hate. I have come to break you away from divisive tendencies of the past which has slowed down our drive to nationhood. I have no enemies to fight. You are all my friends and we share a common destiny"

Goodluck Ebele Jonathan
SEPTEMBER 18, 2010: DECLARATION OF CANDIDACY FOR THE PDP PRESIDENTIAL RACE AT EAGLE SQUARE, ABUJA

The date was May 29, 2011. I had just been sworn in. As the motorcade rode into the villa, I had clear thoughts of the enormity of the challenges facing Nigeria. The expectations of the citizenry arising from our campaign promises, which resonated very well amongst the Nigerian youth, were not lost on me. I was deep in thought on how I would address the challenges of our country and these reflections brought back memories of my political journey.

My entry into Nigerian politics was rather unusual. I still find myself awed at the path it took to get me to the level I had attained. I hobnobbed with politicians in my early forties because the area I come from faced several developmental challenges which I concluded required massive governmental interventions. These politicians were mostly friends and social contacts and though I restrained myself from joining any political party, I found myself increasingly engaged with the political process.

In 1998, as part of General Sani Abacha's transition to civil rule, five political parties were set up. The United Nigeria Congress Party (UNCP) was the biggest one. A friend of mine, late Justice Emmanuel J. Igoniwari, introduced me to late Chief Diepreye Solomon Peter Alamieyeseigha (fondly called DSP) through then Chief Jonathan Kubo (now His Royal Majesty Ibenanaowei of Bassan Clan). I then joined Alamieyeseigha's political team. However, it was not with the intention of contesting for any elective office because I was a civil servant, and was not ready to resign my appointment.

When General Abacha died, his transition programme collapsed. Subsequently, Chief Alamieyeseigha joined the Peoples Democratic Party (PDP) as soon as Abacha's successor, General Abdulsalami Abubakar, cleared the air for political activities. After emerging victorious in the PDP's gubernatorial primaries for Bayelsa State, he invited me to contest with him as his running mate.

I was initially reluctant to accept his offer, but some friends and family members encouraged me to go ahead. Although I will reserve the details of the beginning of my foray into politics for my biography, I will still mention here that among those who persuaded me were late Justice E.J Igoniwari, late Chief Gordon Bozimo, King A.J. Turner and my dear wife, Mrs. Patience Jonathan.

I had my roots in the academia before transiting to the civil service where I worked with the Oil Mineral Producing Areas Development Commission (OMPADEC) as Assistant Director, handling environmental issues. After my initial reluctance, I was persuaded that the offer to serve would afford me the best opportunity to actualise what I believe was good for the people of Bayelsa State.

I took the offer and was up and running as they say. In 1999 I was elected Deputy Governor of Bayelsa State, on the ticket of the Peoples Democratic Party led by its governorship candidate, late Chief Alamieyeseigha. It is unfortunate that due to some political upheavals in the State he lost his job as the Governor, in December 2005. It was an occurrence that elevated me from the Deputy Governor to the office of Governor based on the constitution of Nigeria. I did not plan nor scheme for the position. Similarly, I never contemplated contesting for Vice-Presidency in 2007. I was just one year in as Governor when in December 2006, the PDP presidential primaries held in Abuja. In fact, I had already won the PDP primaries to contest as the Governor of Bayelsa State.

After the Presidential primaries, which Umaru Musa Yar'Adua won, the then President, Chief Olusegun Obasanjo, invited me to the State House. On arrival, I met him seated with Umaru Musa Yar'Adua, the then PDP National Chairman, Dr. Ahmadu Ali and Chief Tony Anenih, a very influential member of the party. These leaders of the party asked me to contest as running mate to Yar'Adua. This was how a man gearing up to contest the gubernatorial election in his state became the Vice Presidential candidate of his party for the 2007 elections. It was a case of divine providence.

The election which brought President Yar'adua and I into office was a watershed in the chequered history of our country, because it was the first time an elected President was handing over to another elected President in a fluid transfer of power. I had come in as a Christian Vice President from the South of Nigeria to serve with a Muslim Northern President. Midway into our administration, unexpected health problems arose with the President, who took ill and became very sick. Now, many who assumed they understood Nigeria would miss the huge implications on that ticket's equation.

The relevance of that equation would not have been that significant if the President's health had held but it became worse, leading to ethno-religious tensions in the country.

Let me say that after we came into office on May 29, 2007, two major issues we had to grapple with were the peace process in the Niger Delta and growing menace of terrorism, driven largely by the radical Islamic terror group, *Jama'atu Ahlis- Sunnah Lidda' Awati Wal Jihad*, popularly known as Boko Haram.

First, our oil production figures were ebbing due to militant activities in the Niger Delta. The Federation distributable accrual was dwindling drastically when we took over due to the crisis in the region and President Yar'Adua, in seeking urgent solutions to increase the revenues of the Federation, offerred amnesty to the militants. One of their demands was that Alamieseigha be released from detention and pardoned by President Yar'Adua. He accepted their terms and mandated me to ensure that my former boss accepted a plea bargain and call the militants to order. President Yar'Adua promised to grant Alamieseigha state pardon if all parties were brought on board to the negotiation table to restore peace in the region

I immediately carried out his instructions. Unfortunately, he passed on before completely fulfilling his promise. When I became President I granted late Alamieseigha a state pardon, in fulfilment of late President Yar'Adua's earlier commitment. Unfortunately this was frowned upon by some of my strongest critics and some went berserk and hurled all manners of insults at me, including accusing me of being 'clannish' for granting State pardon to the former Governor because he was from Bayelsa State. Alamieyeseigha's pardon like every other goodwill gesture I had made, soon became a tool to be used against me by the opposition.

Secondly, the Boko Haram crisis became more intense after the death of their leader (Mohammed Yusuf) while in police custody around July 2009, when I was still the Vice-President. The terrorist sect began to project a more malignant outrage. Our young government had to urgently deal with the extremely dangerous threat the insurgents posed to national security and the well-being of our people. The group continued to expand due to a number of factors which included the instability arising from the Arab Spring, the desire of

Al Qaeda to expand its reach to West Africa (this had been a long term goal of the group's founder, Osama Bin Laden) and also due to home grown support because terror thrives better where there is local support.

While there was not much I could have done between 2007 and 2009 beyond supporting my late boss's initiatives, I had a chance to apply myself to tackling the scourge after I became, first, Acting President, and then after I was sworn in as President, Commander-in-Chief of the Armed Forces of the Federal Republic of Nigeria, in Abuja on May 6, 2010, to complete the late President's tenure which ended on May 29, 2011. In summary, after about one and a half years of service as Governor of Bayelsa State and another three years as the Vice President, following the death of President Yar'Adua, I became President in a complex political atmosphere requiring great tact.

I inherited the administration and promised to continue with the late President's policies on the Niger Delta peace process, tackle corruption, work on the often (rightly) criticized electoral process and fix the country's critical energy problem. I immediately began overhauling and reinventing our security architecture to confront the Boko Haram scourge. I reorganized our security apparatus by re-equipping, training and fully motivating the armed forces afresh.

As I said earlier, Nigeria is a complex society that requires profound knowledge for one to be able to clearly understand its nuanced reality. Northern Nigeria (predominantly Muslim) and Southern Nigeria (predominantly Christian) have had an age long struggle for the control of power in the polity. It is a titanic struggle sewn into the fabric of the Nigerian nation state. I will explain briefly.

When I contested for the 2011 elections with Arc. Namadi Sambo as my running mate, some Northern Nigerian leaders were outraged at my decision to throw my hat into the ring. They claimed that it was their turn to fill the vacancy in the presidency. They raised a smouldering argument over the constitution of my party, the PDP.

On October 6, 2010, a chieftain of the party Alhaji Lawal Kaita, said:
"Anything short of a Northern President is tantamount to stealing our Presidency. Jonathan has to go and he will go.

> *Even if he uses the incumbency power to get his nomination on the platform of the PDP, he will be frustrated out. The North is determined, if that happened, to make the country ungovernable for President Goodluck Jonathan or any other Southerner who finds his way to the seat of power on the platform of the PDP against the principle of the party's zoning policy."*

It was not about Nigeria any longer. The reason they gave was that the government of President Obasanjo, a Southern Christian had just ended after eight years in office. Many Northerners (predominantly core Northern Muslims) voiced out their reservations about my further participation in the race. They wanted me to walk away from my constitutional right. The fact that we came to power on a joint ticket was the truth that was conveniently avoided.

It was a defining moment for our complex nation. This power fault line usually sleeps beneath a lot of pretence. Sadly, it is based on this mendacity that the world sees and assesses Nigeria, our trajectory and the conduct of principal actors in this polity. Our constant discord and disquiet are always traceable to the foundation of Nigeria. Even the name of the country is not native to its people. Of course, our antagonists may ask, what is in a name?

During the 2015 elections, the arguments became further inflamed and intense. Northerners insisted power had been with Southern Christians for about thirteen years and they wanted it back.

President Yar'Adua did not complete the North's term because of his untimely demise which caused very serious tension even among members of my party. Some even went to the ridiculous extent of bringing a case in court to contest my eligibility to run because I took the oath of office as president in 2010 to complete late President Yar'Adua's tenure and again in 2011, after winning the elections. Therefore, they claimed I could not take another oath of office as that would mean doing three terms.

As the storm gathered, intrigue was in abundance. The promoters of regional and religious interests in my party argued that I should not seek re-election. Many were torn between supporting me and standing up for their region and religion, which meant a whole lot to them.

When some individuals preach one Nigeria in public, those who know them better in private simply chuckle. One Nigeria, where there is equity, fairness and justice is what I believe is best for the people of this country. That has been the motivation for all my beliefs and acts. However, the definition of One Nigeria assumes profound differences in the polity. While some people use it as a prop for sloganeering, there are only few who mean it. For some people, one Nigeria is an organism with mutative powers. Nothing is constant. It is a virtual reality device which they alter, degrade and upgrade, depending on the trend of the hour and as it suits their "enlightened" self and group interests.

The intrigue and tension rose roof high, such that those who feigned support for me in public worked against me behind closed doors, very few political intrigues are hidden from a President. Although the conspiracy against my administration was more pronounced in the Northern part of the country, there were also many members of our party in the South that worked against our interest.

Those Northerners who showed open commitment to my cause faced enormous pressure from their various constituencies. This was followed by major and minor betrayals and treachery. Many key party members fell under compulsion to cross over to the opposition party. The pressure was sustained and even increased right into the campaign. By the time of the 2015 elections, it was practically impossible for my supporters in some parts of the North to come out and vote. If you knew anything about elections in Nigeria, you would know that violence plays a massive role in determining who comes out victorious and who loses. Despite my best efforts to produce a free, fair and credible election in 2011, there was still post-election violence that regrettably led to the loss of lives and properties in the North.

Elections in Nigeria come with much violence and vitriol thrown into the political space by otherwise eminent personalities. Brinksmanship is best observed in Nigeria. We are the masters of the game. There were extremely reckless phrases that heated up the political space to the extent that peace was in full flight. This fact supports the argument for the deployment of armed security personnel during elections. The more vociferous antagonists are usually the ones ready with local muscle fully armed for the elections. They would not want armed security personnel to spoil the party. The presence of armed security operatives gives voters the confidence to come out and vote. These are voters who would have stayed home as warned by their neighbourhood thugs.

One of the most traumatizing moments of my Presidency was the cold-blooded murder of innocent members of the National Youth Service Corps (NYSC) in Bauchi State and the near civil war in Kaduna State leading to the death of many and the destruction of properties. This occurred in 2011. I thought long and hard over the needless loss of these lives. It just did not make any sense. How does a parent lose everything like this? How does a nation kill its youth and future in this manner? I still recall the publication of their names in the papers. They were graduates already. The promise of a better tomorrow was very close.

I often wonder why my political philosophy which insists that 'my ambition is not worth the blood of any Nigerian' was not attractive to many amongst our politicians. Threats of violence to 'soak' people in 'blood' were seen as warnings to scare voters away from the polling booth. It was one potent threat everyone knew would be carried out if it caught their fancy. The statement issued before the elections on 'dog and baboon' being soaked in blood, served two purposes. It raised tension before the elections and emboldened wanton destruction and loss of lives afterwards.

If this was excusable, what about the statement issued by the Arewa Consultative Forum (ACF) during the 2015 campaigns? The ACF in a thinly veiled threat had recounted an earlier carnage when it went on to remind everyone of the wanton waste from the post-2011 election violence saying inter alia *"Yoruba suffered N480 billion Naira loss in investments destroyed. Igbo lost N410 billion and the South-South N970 billion...we know these statistics. We have these statistics, so we expect the Igbos to treat our kinsmen as kings and queens".*

A President does not reveal his pain on the saddle no matter how deep it runs, except it is directed at the foundation of the country which he governs and the lives of its citizens become threatened.

Chapter Three

POLITICS AND PATRIOTISM
THE FUEL SUBSIDY DILEMMA

"We are gradually reducing the footprints of government in business activities through privatisation, liberalisation and deregulation based on our recognition that the private sector should be the engine of growth in our economy"

Goodluck Ebele Jonathan
MAY 29, 2012: DEMOCRACY DAY SPEECH

Can an average politician be patriotic? Most citizens of nations are patriotic under certain circumstances but may become unpatriotic in other situations. In Nigeria, during football matches involving the national teams and foreign teams, both Christians and Muslims sing and dance to the tune of the same music. That is patriotism. In politics, I am yet to see such patriotism.

One incident that made me believe that some of our politicians are not patriotic was when I attempted to remove the subsidy on petroleum products. Obviously, people are never happy with the government when the pump price of petroleum products is increased, but the conduct of very senior politicians during that saga was a cause for concern. Sometimes I ask myself if I am satisfied with the type of politics we play in Nigeria.

Politics in Nigeria and some other African nations is conducted like primitive war. All that matters is winning the election. It is so Machiavellian that the end justifies the means. All is deployed, both fair and foul means. In fact, it is like a game without rules. Even in modern warfare, you can be convicted for committing war crimes but in our brand of politics, people believe they can do anything and get away with it.

All over the world, subsidizing hydrocarbons is being discouraged. It does not help the economic growth of oil producing nations. That the Nigerian government-owned refineries are not working optimally is because of the subsidy on petroleum products, a development that discourages private investments.

Subsidy was consuming too much of our revenues. The public believe that the sector was highly corrupt. The then Coordinating Minister of the Economy and Honourable Minister of Finance, Dr. Mrs. Ngozi Okonjo Iweala briefed me about the corrupt practices that a technical committee she had put together discovered. I was alarmed that billions of naira was being lost by the nation through the subsidy regime. I then decided to make that technical committee a Presidential Committee with full powers to summon and arrest. Some recoveries were made but it was still not very satisfactory to me.

Considering the best global practice and the toll subsidy payments were taking on government resources, I felt we had no option than to completely deregulate. It was clear that if government continued to subsidize petroleum products, it would affect economic growth and may even collapse the economy completely. I was of the strong opinion that Nigeria has to devote the bulk of her revenue to capital development.

My thinking was that if we were to continue to grow our economy, we could not afford to devote a major part of our budget to recurrent expenditure, thereby starving all three tiers of government of needed funds.

The issue was discussed at the Executive Council of the Federation meeting. It was resolved that stake holders must be properly briefed, so my team set up various meetings with stakeholders in the last quarter of 2011. The first was with the National Assembly and the second with the State Governors. These were followed up with comprehensive briefings to Labour Unions, Civil Society, Faith-based organisations, Youth groups, Student groups and other non-governmental stakeholders.

I personally attended almost all of the meetings held in *House 7* in the State House except the town hall meeting held in Lagos where the Co-ordinating Minster of the Economy/Finance Minister, Dr. Ngozi Okonjo-Iweala, the Petroleum Minister, Mrs. Diezani Allison-Madueke, the then Governor of the Central Bank of Nigeria, Sanusi Lamido Sanusi (now the Emir of Kano), all spoke on the issue of subsidy.

We held several meetings with State Governors. At one of these meetings, it was agreed that the Governors would conduct town hall meetings and media enlightenment campaigns in their various States.

The State Governors needed additional money to boost their receivables from the federation accounts. They wanted subsidy removal to commence immediately. But I objected. They agreed when I explained that end of the year activities including Christmas and New Year celebrations usually bring a lot of financial pressure on Nigerians. I then advised that since there would be no provision for subsidy in the 2012 budget, it would be better to start the complete deregulation from January 2012.

Definitely, January was not the best month to announce the deregulation. However, if we did not announce the removal in January, how would the product importers be paid, since, the 2012 budget proposal made no provision for subsidy? I could not countenance in my conscience extra budgetary payments.

The announcement was eventually made on January 1, 2012. Understandably, a lot of people who went home for the Christmas and New Year holidays were affected due to the increment in fares following the adjustment of the pump price by marketers. Almost immediately, organised protests erupted in some states including Abuja. The demonstrations began mostly in states controlled by the opposition.

Even Nigerian Labour Unions that were exhaustively consulted joined the protests. Also, some sections of Civil Society that were properly briefed which we thought would go along with the idea joined the protests. The then main opposition party had a field day. In fact, security reports I received showed clearly that they instigated the protests.

In Lagos State for instance, it was like a carnival. Musicians, comedians, and other celebrities were engaged by opposition elements to join the protests. Refreshments were served to protesters. Every morning Lagos State Government workers cleaned up the Gani Fawehinmi Park and prepared it for the day's protest. It appeared as though the protesters were very special guests of the Lagos State Government. Similar scenarios played out in other opposition controlled states.

State Governors of the main opposition party, some of whom were champions of the subsidy removal in our meetings on the matter, made a volte face! They saw the subsidy removal as a very good opportunity to bring my government down and clear their path to power. Politics has a way of letting you know the inner recess of the human mind.

I recall vividly that at one of the meetings we had with the Governors at the Council Chambers, Mr. Adams Oshiomhole, then Governor of Edo Sate, showed his displeasure towards his colleagues. To his credit, he was the only opposition Governor who stood by what we agreed. He told his colleagues that it was not fair for them to turn against the President when they even wanted the deregulation to have started months earlier.

The House of Representatives whose Speaker, then Rt. Hon. Aminu Waziri Tambuwal, was hobnobbing with the opposition (he eventually defected to the opposition) did not help matters. Thinking that I had left the country for South Africa to attend the centenary celebration of the African National Congress (ANC), Speaker Tambuwal convened the House to sit on a Sunday just to condemn the deregulation. That was the first and only time in Nigeria's political history that the Parliament sat on a Sunday. At that sitting an opposition member of the House got up to allege that I had abandoned the nation at such a crucial time to join in festivities in South Africa.

Unknown to the House, on that same day while they were sitting, I was at Eagle Square to commission Mass Transit vehicles my administration purchased to cushion the effect of subsidy removal. I had to address the issue by telling the nation that it was untrue that I abandoned the situation at hand to go to South Africa. The country was tense and the public was wondering what would happen next.

On one of those tense days, some Christian clerics met with me in the evening to discuss the issue. They pleaded that I should rescind the deregulation because of the impending crisis they envisaged. They told me that if I continued with the deregulation, I will be pushed out of power by the people.

I thanked them and told them clearly that I was not going to pull back because if I did not deregulate, the economy would crash, and the people would still push me out of power. I noted that it will be more honourable for me to deregulate and let the people push me out. My successor would still have to deregulate, otherwise he would not even be able to pay salaries. At that point Nigerians would appreciate the decision I took. I was willing to give up power to ensure that the right thing was done.

Those who met with me included: His Eminence, Rt. Rev. Nicholas D. Okoh, Primate of the Anglican Church, His Eminence Dr. Sunday Ola Makinde, Prelate of the Methodist Church of Nigeria, Dr. Emma Dzzigau, President of HEKAN, Rev. Dr. William Okoye, General Overseer All Christian Fellowship Mission, Rev. Emeka Nwankpa, General Overseer Chapel of Faith Bible Assembly International , Ven. Obioma Onwuzurumba, the Villa Chaplain, Pastor Abba Mshelia, the administrator of the Villa Chapel, Rev. P.J. A. Olaiya, President Living Faith foundation, Kaduna and John Kennedy Opara, Executive Secretary Nigerian Christian Pilgrims

Commission.

That same evening, Bishop David Oyedepo, General Overseer, Living Faith Mission (Winners Chapel) also came to see me on the same issue. I explained to him why the issue of deregulation was inevitable for the country.

The protests continued unabated. In all of these, one woman I pitied most was my aged mother who was with me in the State House. Everyday, she watched on televison, protesters carrying a casket with my picture on it, and having the inscription RIP (rest in peace). I could imagine her trauma. This is a woman who had had ten live births with only my elder sister and I surviving.

The leaders of Nigerian youth groups were forthright on the fuel subsidy issue. They were briefed just like other stakeholders. To their credit no youth or student group joined the protests. Young people were nonetheless recruited individually to join the protests, but not under the banner of any group. That helped to minimize the impact of the protests. I have stated that Africa's hope lies in her next generation of leaders. The behaviour of these youth groups vindicates my opinion.

I have to thank the 7th Senate of the Federal Republic of Nigeria led by Senator David Mark for their contribution in ending the protests. They held meetings with Labour and Civil Society leaders and other interest groups.

The Senate's intervention led to a robust negotiation with these leaders and finally, a middle course was agreed. The pump price of premium motor spirit, (petrol/gasoline), was moved to 97 Naira per litre. When the international price of crude oil came down, we further reduced the pump price to 87 Naira per litre. Interestingly, at that time, the opposition insisted that the price of petrol must be reduced further to reflect the margin of drop in world crude prices.

When the opposition took over power, they tinkered with deregulation but finally increased the price of petrol from N87 to N145. Even when the international price of crude oil fell, the price of petrol remained the same despite claims from the camp of the opposition during the electioneering campaigns that it should sell for far less than the price they met. However, it still gives me some succour that the Buhari administration took this decision soon after taking over the reins of power as I had predicted my successors would do.

It made me remember what I told the clergymen that the person who would take over from me was going to deregulate and that the protests were politically motivated. For the new government to attempt deregulation shows that they knew the positive effects deregulation would bring to the economy, yet they hired protesters against my government. This is quite disturbing. Does it then mean that politicians cannot be patriotic? Must we play politics with issues of national development?

We knew that with deregulation, the transportation cost would be quite heavy on Nigerians. To reduce this burden, we started discussing with a group led by Ben Murray-Bruce (now a Senator) on the possibilities of direct subsidy to commuters but since the deregulation did not succeed, that discussion was aborted half way. Since the government did not completely deregulate and the pump price was fixed at 97 Naira per litre, it prompted an increase in that year's budget by 161 billion naira in order to accommodate the partial subsidy.

Even at that, the government was able to save some money. The Federal, State and Local Governments shared the gains from moving the pump price from 65 Naira per litre to 97 Naira per litre. These savings at the Federal Government level were pooled into a Subsidy Reinvestment and Empowerment Programme (SURE-P).

Under this programme young people were recruited across the country to maintain roads and other public infrastructure while conditional cash grants were given to pregnant women. When the Economist magazine noted that Nigeria's GDP grew at above 6% from 2012, this empowerment programme played a huge role in that development. The SURE-P programme was headed by Dr. Christopher Kolade, a highly respected Nigerian and later General Martin Luther Agwai who was Kolade's deputy.

To further justify my belief that some Nigerian politicians find it difficult to be patriotic, in Ngozi Okonjo-Iweala's book, *Fighting Corruption is Dangerous: The Stories Behind the Headlines*, she noted that the former Governor of Cross River State, Mr. Donald Duke approached her and asked her not to serve in my government so that the government will not succeed.

It is sad to think that this was a government that had just been elected to serve for a four year term and some people were already plotting its failure, just to enable them win the next election. It is worrisome. Do they consider their people's welfare when they make such Machiavellian calculations?

You can imagine the pain and hardship a failed government can cause the nation for four years in terms of businesses that would collapse and the citizenry that will be impoverished. The number of people who will lose their jobs, the number of children that cannot go to school, the hordes of Nigerians that will die because they cannot pay their medical bills amongst others. Still, some people wanted the government to fail for no other reason than their personal political ambition.

Until African politicians consider their countries' interest first in whatever they do, the continent will continue to lag behind. Politics should be about the people and not about fighting to occupy offices.

Chapter Four

THE CHIBOK SCHOOL GIRLS AFFAIR

"We must never allow contestation for political office to degenerate to a level where it becomes a threat to our nation's peace, security and stability"

Goodluck Ebele Jonathan
APRIL 8, 2011: DURING THE INAUGURATION OF THE
OHAFIA ARMY BARRACKS IN ABIA STATE

Our nation and citizens faced a cascade of challenges between 2011 and 2015 most of which were avoidable. The worst was the menace of the radical Islamic terror sect, Boko Haram, with their mindless destruction, insane mass killings, utter savagery, kidnapping of innocent children, women, men and other despicable acts of brutality.

However, nothing they did quite got the attention of the international community like the abduction of school girls from Government Girls Secondary School, Chibok.

The sequences of the sad and unfortunate events are as follow:

Monday, April 15, 2014
01:00 Hours

The notification came that heavily armed Boko Haram Islamists had arrived in an open truck and quietly abducted about 276 girls from Government Girls Secondary School, Chibok, Borno State in North-Eastern Nigeria, which is about two hours drive from Nigeria's border with Cameroon.

On that fateful night, as students slept in their dormitories, gunmen invaded the school and abducted over two hundred girls in an open truck. The regular activities at the school had come to a halt because of the danger posed by Boko Haram terrorists. However, some students were asked to stay behind because of the ongoing Senior Secondary School Certificate Examinations (SSCE). They were supposed to take their physics paper the next day.

As the President and as a parent, I could and can empathise with the emotional trauma the parents of these girls had been put through by the experience. My wife and I were devastated on receiving the intelligence report even before the rest of the nation knew about it. We were in shock. I had to jolt myself out of my state of shock to take stock of what happened and why it occured but it was not so easy for my wife who was very emotional about the whole incident.

I was briefed that the security personnel on ground had taken immediate action to rescue the girls. In the morning, I sent for the Chief of Defence Staff

(CDS), Chief of Army Staff and Chief of Air Staff for a preliminary evaluation of the incident. On 17 April, three days after the abduction, there was still no positive news on the whereabouts or rescue of the girls.

I summoned the Service Chiefs and other military and intelligence top brass to a meeting at the Presidential Villa where they laid out their strategic plans to rescue the girls. I also sought answers to burning questions in my mind.

Why and how did this happen? These were innocent teenagers. Why did the State Governor not provide security for the school as he had promised after he rejected the advice of the Federal Government not to hold examinations in Chibok and instead move the girls to more secured centres? The Governors of the other two States facing similar fate heeded the advice by relocating children from the affected schools. If the children must stay behind in line with the position of Borno State Government, why didn't the State Governor make arrangements to protect the school children?

Before April, the terrorists had struck in schools in Yobe and heinously murdered over fifty school boys and this had been the catalyst for our request to the State Governments in the three states mostly affected by the crisis to move their examination centres to safe zones.

In Nigeria, secondary schools are constitutionally the responsibility of the State Governments. The Federal Government can only recommend but cannot compel State Governments to act with regard to secondary schools other than the Federal Government owned Unity Schools (Federal Government Colleges). The Chibok incident was most puzzling because the North-East, which was the heartland of the terrorists, was where we had a very strong military presence on the ground. That was the more reason why the revolting development was very disturbing. I began to question why these girls were abducted in the night and taken away in an open truck. My curiosity was further aroused by the information that the girls were taken away in a very swift manner and there were no reports of gunshots.

My mind was ravaged by a torrent of questions: Where were the school matrons, security guards, teachers and the principal? I made enquiries as to where the principal of the school at the time of the incident was and I was informed that she had a scheduled medical appointment at Maiduguri, the State capital, on the same day the girls were abducted. Why would adults leave such vulnerable young girls all on their own particularly in Borno State, the base of the Boko Haram sect well known for its rabid anti-Western education posture, especially towards girls.

As if on cue, protests broke out within days. They were neatly choreographed and nicely distributed around the country, popping up like poxes on a body infested with chicken pox. Anyone who knows the nature of protests would see through these actions. Yes, many joined of their own freewill out of genuine concern and sympathy for the girls and their parents but at the heart of the protests was a certain degree of premeditation.

The swiftness of the protests and its organization was just a matter of politicians seizing a rare opportunity to politicise an unfortunate incident.

When the girls had still not been found two weeks after the military launched their rescue mission, I summoned the State commissioner for education, the school principal and State Commissioner of police in a bid to get to the root of the matter. The rescue of the girls was paramount to me. We needed to rescue them from the ordeal, unite them with their families and show the insurgents that my government would not give up on education in the North particularly for girls. However, none of those I summoned could provide anything tangible by way of useful information.

In addition to what the regular intelligence services were doing, I set up a team headed by retired Brigadier-General Ibrahim Sabo, which included security officials and civil society members including the National Council of Women Societies, to go to Borno state to investigate and brief me. They also could not bring substantial information that could help in rescuing the girls. This is what defines the folly of those who questioned our pace and commitment. A better word would be gambit; a calculated move to place the administration in the direct path of national and global odium. To an extent, it worked especially with those who would applaud anything against the Jonathan administration.

While we strategized on possible ways to rescue the girls, the opposition worked up groups and interests in a festival of protests. They maximized the mileage offered by the situation. The hashtag #bringbackourgirls suddenly became a cause celebre. Everybody from page boy to mother of the day, wanted in on the ride.

It was not long before it popped up on the White House lawn, with the then United States First Lady, Mrs. Michelle Obama, bearing a bring-back-our-girls banner.

Even when I attended South African President, Jacob Zuma's inauguration ceremony for his second term, the Master of Ceremony dredged up the #bringbackourgirls hashtag. The strange thing was that all of the protests were entirely directed at me rather than the State Governor whose responsibility it was to provide first line security for the school as the chief security officer of the State. Such is the awesome power of psychological programming.

The electorate was programmed to see my administration as the villain. If someone was conducting an experiment on how propaganda could be used to bring down a government, it worked. It was a roaring success. Only it did not work without a very expansive conspiracy network, the consequence of which was too costly in lives and limbs.

The Chibok Girls incident happened under my watch. As President, the buck stopped at my table and I must take responsibility. However, for the Federal Government to succeed, the co-operation from the state is paramount but we did not get that from Borno State. How could the State have rejected the request from the Federal Government to relocate the students?

So, who or what is Boko Haram? Boko Haram as generally referenced to literally mean 'Western education' is a taboo. The real name is *Jama'atu Ahlis Sunnah Lidda' Awati Wal Jihad*, meaning: Those who uphold the teachings of the prophet and crusade.

At this juncture, it may be prudent to state that one of their demands was that I should abandon my Christian faith and accept Islam. In other words, they wanted a Muslim President for Nigeria amongst others. It is evident that Boko Haram is a group of terrorists who hide under the influence of Islam to achieve their own personal and group goals which are not only heinous and dastardly but also political. They are well funded, in view of the sophistication and magnitude of their operations.

Some of their funding come from bank raids, ransom from kidnapping, extortion and other criminal revenue generation means, but they have other sources of funding because the aforementioned alone cannot account for the sheer scale of their operations. There is evidence that they also get funding from some wealthy individuals who wholly or in part support their Jihadi intentions. They operate in a similar fashion to ISIS and Al Qaeda. Boko Haram even changed its name officially to ISIS West and Central Africa in May 2015 (See Annex).

In the meantime, the disappearance of these teenagers raised more questions as time went on, but we were focused on how best to rescue them. The Governor of the State (a member of the opposition party), rather than join the Federal Government in the efforts to rescue the girls opted to stage a cross-continent roadshow in Europe and America, addressing foreign media when the issue that was burning was in his home state and the attention of the world was locked on Nigeria.

All the nineteen governors of Northern Nigeria had been invited to a meeting with the then US National Security Adviser to Obama, Susan Rice, at the White House on March 18, 2014. A few weeks before the Chibok girls were kidnapped. At that meeting, the Borno State Governor vehemently made spurious claims about my administration that he had to be cautioned by his Gombe State counterpart, Alhaji Ibrahim Dankwanbo.

It is instructive that apart from a few habitual agitators and regular activists, some of the leaders of the #bringbackourgirls movement were mostly key members of the opposition who had a view to a future reward. On October 16, 2014, Chief Audu Ogbeh a chieftain of the All Progressive Congress (APC), who later became a minister, had said on camera at an APC rally at the Eagle Square Abuja, *"I want to thank members of the #BringBackOurGirls group which is being led by members of our party."*

The people of Chibok were not part of the initial wave of protests as they were more concerned with working with the Federal Government on the efforts to rescue their daughters. That was of some import. The Western media was pouring vitriol on our administration. We were presented as the problem of Nigeria far beyond the Chibok issue. They made it a point that they were only interested in regime change. If the Jonathan administration goes and the opposition comes, the security challenges posed by Boko Haram will vanish, the Chibok girls will be rescued and the country will be better off, it was echoed. Of course, it was a deliberate attempt to distort history and build faulty premises to worsen Nigeria's future.

The tactical attacks by the Obama administration were many. They refused to provide any real military backing or equipment to aid the rescue of the Chibok girls, citing the Leahy Law which they claimed prevented them from supporting any military that was engaged in human rights abuses, but this law did not stop them from assisting the armed forces of Nigeria's neighbours who had been accused of serious human rights violations.

The hash-taggers and crucify campaigners did not stop to ask the Governor why he insisted the girls remain in that danger zone. Apart from few voices which were drowned, no one was interested in knowing why the girls were left alone in the school despite the Federal Government advice to the contrary. How does a State Governor at a time like that fail to question this obvious dereliction of duty and make little or no efforts at coordinating the rescue efforts? The object was not the truth about what happened but how what happened could be a tool in the hands of the opposition. Many individuals and groups were playing various roles from different perspectives, mostly for their own self interest and not that of the school girls.

In fact, Alhaji Lai Mohammed the then opposition mouthpiece was agitated at some point when it seemed the girls had been found. On October 16, 2014, he said:

> *"It is clear that President Jonathan has suddenly shown more interest in their release after his consensus nomination as PDP candidate for next year's elections. Our appeal, therefore, is for the President to allow the immediate release of the girls rather than wait for when it will give maximum boost to his political fortunes."*

Mr. Mohammed also alleged that my administration was behind the abduction, saying:

> *"The same Government that is apparently behind the activities (Boko Haram's activities) had bluntly ignored wise counsel and said it will never negotiate their release."*

At a point, the entire campaign of the opposition was riding on the girls. I thought these people could even pray that the girls stayed wherever they were until they were through with their scheming. It was however not surprising that some leaders of the #bringbackourgirls movement were rewarded with promotions and appointments shortly after the general elections. In fact, Hadiza Bala Usman, one of the co-founders of the #bringbackourgirls Movement was appointed the Managing Director of the Nigerian Ports Authority (NPA) in July 2016.

The criticism over alleged slow response was one of those absurd injections into the discourse, but when it comes from eminent persons who were supposed to be circumspect; it began to look more plausible to observers. My administration was not slow in responding to the Chibok incident. How could response have been slow in a military occupied zone? Before the Presidency was alerted by the intelligence services, the military were already on it. As soon as I got the intelligence report, I summoned the service chiefs for briefing. I was informed that the Air Force was already using several surveillance aircraft to search the area.

Again, I was accused of not visiting Chibok immediately after the abduction of the girls. A lot of assumptions were made. What was not countenanced was the fact that a President moved with security advice from experts because he ceases to be a private citizen the moment he wears the powers of state. For the avoidance of doubt, let me state that I had made up my mind to visit Chibok even against the advice of my Service Chiefs and sent an advance party to the area in preparation for my visit. It was meant to be an unannounced visit. However someone in the know, most likely a saboteur, leaked the information to the Western media and they reported it.

Of course when it became public knowledge that I planned to visit Chibok, the security chiefs requested the trip to be cancelled. Their advice was germane and regrettably, my visit had to be cancelled. Sometime, in the heat of the moment, one got the impression that I was being goaded to appear there in the great expectation of something untoward happening to me. I was to access Chibok in a helicopter that would have flown over Boko Haram infested areas.

This wave of misinformation on the kidnap of the Chibok girls is similar to the malicious propaganda still being spread by those who saw nothing commendable in all we did to curb the Boko Haram situation in the North East. They claimed that I left several local government areas under the control of the insurgents. Fortunately, the Nigeria military had successfully liberated most of the local governments in the North East from the insurgents; a situation that made it possible for INEC to organise elections in all the affected areas. The towns and communities liberated before the 2015 elections include Bama, Dikwa, Buni Yadi, Baga, Konduga, Madagali, Mubi, Gamboru-Ngala, Michika, Damboa, Monguno, Gwoza, Marte, Gujba, Bara, Hong, Kukawa, Goniri, Askira and Abadam.

We did everything humanly possible to locate the girls. I wrote letters to the Presidents of the United States, Barack Obama, Prime Minister of the United Kingdom, David Cameron, President of France, Francois Hollande as well as leaders of China, Israel and our neighbouring countries for help. They supported the search in their different ways and capacities but until I left offfice, it was all to no avail. On several occasions when raids were conducted and news of rescue of hostages filtered in, my hopes were raised but almost immediately dashed when victims were processed and none of the Chibok girls were among those rescued.

As an aside, while thanking the men and women of the US security services who were deployed to Nigeria and toiled day and night in the Northeast in search of the Chibok Girls, my surprise at the role played by the then U.S. President Barack Obama, still calls to doubt his genuine intentions for Nigeria.

For some strange reasons, the Obama administration had tactically pencilled Nigeria and my administration for failure. Amongst many manoeuvres, was the refusal to provide any real military backing to Nigeria's Armed Forces. President Obama and his security adviser, Susan Rice, bluntly refused to sell any military hardware including jet fighters and attack helicopters to Nigeria. Obama cited the Leahy Law as the reason his regime prevented the American Government from supporting Nigeria in providing weapons to fight Boko Haram. Even when the State of Israel expressed the willingness to sell attack helicopters to Nigeria, the gesture was frustrated by the Obama administration that kept waving the same Leahy Law like a banner.

My administration, including a team of international partners with their respective governments, devoted considerable amount of resources in the search and rescue of the girls.

I believe one day some of the security experts and actors that were involved in the search and rescue will tell the world the truth about the kidnap of the Chibok school girls.

I am glad that at the time of writing this book, some of them have been found and I hope the rest of the girls will be found and re-united with their families.

Chapter Five

CORRUPTION AND THE BLAME GAME

"For you to solve corruption problem you must use modern technologies to prevent people from stealing and that is what we are working on."

Goodluck Ebele Jonathan
JANUARY 12, 2015 ADDRESS TO PARTY SUPPORTERS AT THE
PDP CAMPAIGN RALLY IN IBADAN, OYO STATE

Corruption is as old as independent Nigeria. That is why all military takeovers of governments since the January 15 1966 coup had always been justified on the basis of ridding the country of corruption. Every successive administration has fought corruption one way or the other but the scourge still remains.

In a lecture delivered by Bishop Matthew Hassan Kukah, at the Platform, Covenant Centre, Lagos, on October 1, 2015, the inimitable Bishop of the Sokoto Diocese of the Catholic Church captured this flawed perception succinctly. He said:

> *"The question we should be asking ourselves now is, how and why is it that every coup plotter in Nigeria hung his colours on the mast of fighting corruption? How come that all successive governments have come in, accusing their predecessors of massive corruption only to turn around and do even worse or leave a similar legacy of rut?"*

The January 15, 1966 coup led by Major Kaduna Nzeogwu and which introduced the military into politics, cited the following as the reason for overthrowing leaders of the First Republic:

> *"Our enemies are the political profiteers, the swindlers, the men in high and low places that seek bribes and demand 10 per cent; those that seek to keep the country divided permanently so that they can remain in office as ministers or VIPs at least, the tribalists, the nepotists, those that make the country look big for nothing before international circles, those that have corrupted our society and put the Nigerian political calendar back by their words and deeds."*

General Yakubu Gowon who took over following the tragic end of Major General Johnson Aguiyi-Ironsi, who eventually led the first military junta after the Nzeogwu coup, noted emphatically that the nation was drifting towards destruction because of lack of trust, unity, and sense of purpose. In his inaugural speech, Gowon stated:

> "Suffice it to say that, putting all considerations to test-political, economic, as well as social-the base for unity is not there or is so badly rocked, not only once but several times. I therefore feel that we should review the issue of our national standing and see if we can help stop the country from drifting away into utter destruction."

According to Gowon, he was on a mission to redirect the country *"in accordance with an all-round code of good conduct and etiquette"*. The echo of a drifting nation requiring urgent change in a new direction again resurrected in the voice of Brigadier Murtala Ramat Muhammed, who overthrew Gowon in July, 1975.

In his maiden broadcast to the nation on July 29, 1975, Brigadier Muhammed accused Gen. Gowon of not only failing as a corrective regime but also plunging the nation into chaos. Accusing the administration of Gowon of indecision and indiscipline, Muhammed said:

> "Fellow Nigerians, events of the past few years have indicated that despite our great human and material resources, the Government has not been able to fulfill the legitimate expectations of our people. Nigeria has been left to drift. This situation, if not arrested, would inevitably have resulted in chaos and even bloodshed.
>
> In the endeavour to build a strong, united and virile nation, Nigerians have shed much blood. The thought of further bloodshed, for whatever reasons must, I am sure, be revolting to our people. The Armed Forces, having examined the situation, came to the conclusion that certain changes were inevitable.
>
> After the civil war, the affairs of state, hitherto a collective responsibility became characterized by lack of consultation, indecision, indiscipline and even neglect. Indeed, the public at large became disillusioned and disappointed by these developments. This trend was clearly incompatible with the philosophy and image of a corrective regime. Unknown to the

> *general public, the feeling of disillusionment was also evident among members of the armed forces whose administration was neglected but who, out of sheer loyalty to the Nation, and in the hope that there would be a change, continued to suffer in silence...*
>
> *The leadership, either by design or default, had become too insensitive to the true feelings and yearnings of the people. The nation was thus plunged inexorably into chaos. It was obvious that matters could not, and should not, be allowed in this manner, and in order to give the nation a new lease of life, and sense of direction..."*

Gen. Muhammed's administration was also cut short when the Head of State was killed by another band of military adventurers led by Colonel Buka Suka Dimka. Although Dimka's coup of February 13, 1976 was aborted, he still managed to tell the nation in a broadcast that the reasons of corruption, incompetence and maladministration for which Gowon was overthrown persisted in Muhammed's time.

In a second speech which Colonel Dimka was said to have prepared but never got the opportunity to present to Nigerians, he further explained:

> *"We the Young Revolutionaries have once again taken over the government to save Murtala from total disgrace and prevent him from committing further blunders and totally collapsing the country before he runs away in the name of retirement to enjoy the huge fortune he got through bribe which he has now stored outside this country."*

When Gen. Olusegun Obasanjo took over government in 1976 after the assassination of Muhammed he made it clear that his administration would fight corruption and focus on instilling a *"new sense of public morality among all classes of Nigerians."* In his maiden speech, Obasanjo warned that he would not tolerate inefficiency or improper conduct from those entrusted with public office, saying:

> *"We shall be severe in our dealing with foreign and Nigerian*

profiteers who try to stand in the way of our policy to free our economy and improve the lot of the ordinary and deprived citizenry of this country. I expect every public officer indeed, every Nigerian to measure up to a high degree of efficiency, integrity and moral rectitude. The purge of the public service of undesirable elements was undertaken to revitalize the service.

This objective has not been fully achieved. Those that are diligent and honest in their work need not fear. Indeed they would be rewarded. But those who continue to be indolent, inefficient or corrupt will be removed. These standards are set not only for public servants but for all Nigerians."

The military junta headed by Gen. Muhammadu Buhari which overthrew President Shagari's administration jailed people from between fifty to three hundred years on charges of corruption.

In the speech announcing the overthrow of the the democratically elected government of President Shehu Shagari, Brig. Sani Abacha also placed justification for the coup on the doorsteps of corruption, saying;

"...our leaders revel in squandermania, corruption and indiscipline, and continue to proliferate public appointments in complete disregard of our stark economic realities. After due consultations over these deplorable conditions, I and my colleagues in the armed forces have in the discharge of our national role as promoters and protectors of our national interest decided to effect a change in the leadership of the government of the Federal Republic of Nigeria and form a Federal Military Government....."

Similarly, on his first broadcast to Nigerians after he emerged as the Head of State, Buhari said;

"....While corruption and indiscipline have been associated with our state of under-development; these two evils in our body politics have attained unprecedented height in the past few years.

The corrupt, inept and insensitive leadership in the last four years has been the source of immorality and impropriety in our society. Since what happens in any society is largely a reflection of the leadership of that society, we deplore corruption in all its facets. This government will not tolerate kick-backs, inflation of contracts and over-invoicing of imports etc. Nor will it condone forgery, fraud, embezzlement, misuse and abuse of office and illegal dealings in foreign exchange and smuggling."

On August 27, 1985 Brigadier General Dogon Yaro announced the overthrow of the administration of Gen. Buhari. However, it was Gen. Ibrahim Babangida, who later emerged as the new Head of State and gave details of why Buhari was overthrown, stressing that his administration had derailed, was completely alienated from the people and continued with the mismanagement of the nation's leadership. Here are excerpts from Babangida's maiden broadcast to the nation:

"Since January 1984, however, we have witnessed a systematic denigration of that hope. It was stated then that mismanagement of political leadership and a general deterioration in the standard of living, which had subjected the common man to intolerable suffering, were the reasons for the intervention.

Nigerians have since then been under a regime that continued with those trends. Events today indicate that most of the reasons which justified the military takeover of government from the civilians still persist.

The initial objectives were betrayed and fundamental changes do not appear on the horizon. Because the present state of uncertainty, suppression and stagnation resulted from the perpetration of a small group, the Nigerian Armed Forces could not as a part of that government be unfairly committed to take responsibility for failure.

Our dedication to the cause of ensuring that our nation

remains a united entity worthy of respect and capable of functioning as a viable and credible part of the international community dictated the need to arrest the situation…

Let me at this point attempt to make you understand the premise upon which it became necessary to change the leadership. The principles of discussions, consultation and co-operation which should have guided decision-making process of the Supreme Military Council and the Federal Executive Council were disregarded soon after the government settled down in 1984. Where some of us thought it appropriate to give a little more time, anticipating a conducive atmosphere that would develop, in which affairs of state could be attended to with greater sense of responsibility, it became increasingly clear that such expectations could not be fulfilled…

Regrettably, it turned out that Major-General Muhammadu Buhari was too rigid and uncompromising in his attitudes to issues of national significance. Efforts to make him understand that a diverse polity like Nigeria required recognition and appreciation of differences in both cultural and individual perceptions, only served to aggravate these attitudes…

And so it came to be that the same government which received the tumultuous welcome now became alienated from the people. To prevent a complete erosion of our given mandate therefore, we had to act so that hope may be rebuilt.

While this government recognises the bitterness created by the irresponsible excesses of the politicians, we consider it unfortunate that methods of such nature as to cause more bitterness were applied to deal with past misdeeds. We must never allow ourselves to lose our sense of natural justice. The innocent cannot suffer the crimes of the guilty. The guilty should be punished only as a lesson for the future. In line with this government's intention to uphold fundamental human rights, the issue of detainees will be looked into with dispatch.

> *The last twenty months have not witnessed any significant changes in the national economy. Contrary to expectations, we have so far been subjected to a steady deterioration in the general standard of living; and intolerable suffering by the ordinary Nigerians have risen higher, scarcity of commodities has increased, hospitals still remain mere consulting clinics, while educational institutions are on the brink of decay. Unemployment has stretched to critical dimensions..."*

Immediately after the 2011 elections, my administration was repeatedly accused of being corrupt. Despite the blackmail, I remained committed to combating corruption in a systemic way, knowing it was endemic. We vigorously devised and implemented a thorough and strategic plan to fight corruption, using technology, albeit within the context of the rule of law and due process.

Before I go deeper into this, let me address a false narrative my detractors have used to besmirch my name. They claim that I once said that 'stealing is not corruption'. This is not true. Following the constant stigmatisation of Nigerians as corrupt, I invited the leadership of the legislature and judiciary to a meeting.

In attendance were the Senate President and his Deputy, Speaker of the House of Representatives and his Deputy; the Chief Justice of Nigeria (CJN), the President of the Court of Appeal, the Chief Judge of the Federal High Court and six States' Chief Judges from each of the six geopolitical zones. Also invited were heads of the two anti-corruption agencies viz, the Chairman of Economic and Financial Crimes Commission (EFCC) and Chairman of the Independent Corrupt Practices and Other related Offences Commission (ICPC). I presided over the meeting with the Vice President.

My thinking was that the executive arm of government alone could not effectively eradicate the scourge of corruption, hence the need for that meeting. I personally appealed to them and argued that only an all-inclusive approach could bring about tangible successes in the anti-corruption fight. The judiciary, the legislative and the executive arms of government needed to join forces if we were to end the theft of public resources and stop corruption. I went on to methodically present my case as follow:

- I propose that we work together to curb corruption.
- When matters of corruption are presented to the courts, there would be no effective results if they were not treated in a painstaking and timely manner.
- The parliament needs to play a fundamental role in passing strong and effective laws. When laws are weak, the judiciary would not be able to do much.

The then Chief Justice of Nigeria, Honourable Justice Dahiru Musdapher, in his contributions acknowledged that he was of the same opinion. He added that because of the perception of corruption in Nigeria he had to isolate all the case files before the Supreme Court having to do with corruption charges. He said that after reading through those files, he discovered that more than 70% were not corruption cases, per se, but crimes of stealing. The individuals involved were however not charged to court for stealing but rather in preparing the case files, the prosecutors used the term "corruption".

It was on the strength of his submission that I expounded to say that we should stop calling a spade an agricultural implement. Corruption does not fully capture the act of stealing. A person can indeed be corrupt without stealing a dime. Those who are incapable of comprehending this elevated thought and the mischievous crowd, go about claiming till date, that I said 'stealing is not corruption.' They never bothered to even check the context in which I spoke. If you ask many of those clinging to that falsehood and mouthing the malicious misrepresentation, to quote where I said it, they will tell you 'they only heard.'

Let me categorically state that I have never said stealing is good and that people should steal, neither did the CJN. Stealing is stealing and instead of calling it corruption, let us call the thief by his proper name and not use a blanket word like corruption.

Corruption encompasses many things. According to Transparency International, corruption is defined as the 'abuse of entrusted power for private gain'. The Merriam Webster's dictionary defines stealing as 'to take without permission or legal right and without intending to return'. If a government minister upon a cabinet dissolution takes a vehicle that he is not entitled to and converts it to personal use then that is stealing. We must not lump everything together and say stealing is corruption. We must isolate stealing and make it as plain as day because Nigerians hate thieves. I abhor jungle justice, but we have witnessed Nigerians show their hatred for suspected thieves by burning them alive.

It is important also to note how we supported the institutional development of secure systems and mechanisms, to curb corruption in public service and plug revenue leakages. My administration spearheaded the development of the Treasury Single Account (TSA), the Integrated Personnel and Payroll Information System (IPPIS) and the Bank Verification Number (BVN).

No administration can either be entirely bad or perfect. Good governance is a process. Rather than media hype or arresting and parading suspected offenders on television, my strategy was to strengthen our public institutions and law enforcement agencies to prevent people from defrauding the system ab initio.

Let me explain how we went about doing this, using the corruption in the fertilizer sector as an example. My experience as Deputy Governor, and Governor of Bayelsa State, as well as Vice-President and President of the Federal Republic of Nigeria had exposed me to the challenges in the fertilizer sector. We did extensive research and finally were able to establish how the States and Federal Government were spending billions of Naira on the fertilizer regime but only about 11% or less of the fertilizer subsidy benefitted the end users- Nigerian farmers.

It became more apparent that the remaining 90% were either being stolen or siphoned out of the country through clever schemes. It was not easy, but we came in, took action and cleaned it up. Coincidentally, my Minister of Agriculture, Dr. Akinwumi Adesina, did his PhD research work on fertilizer distribution in West Africa. His knowledge of the field came in handy in our quest to curb the fraud.

We developed what we called the Electronic Wallet. This was a policy that cut out the middle man and got millions of farmers to register for the e-wallet using their cell phones from which they received text alerts directly from the ministry, telling them where to pick up their fertilizer, and how much to pay.

Text messaging system that directs genuine farmers to pick up fertilizers and seeds. This system was designed when I became President to eliminate the grand corruption that riddled the fertilizer distribution system.. The system worked and farmers where better off, while government saved huge sums of money.

According to Velocity Capital, a Dutch private equity firm, in their independent assessment showed that, the electronic wallet initiative of the Federal Ministry of Agriculture and Rural Development under the Growth Enhancement Support Scheme (GESS), had saved the Federal Government of Nigeria over $192 million by 2012, the first year in which it was introduced.

My administration developed and implemented the Integrated Personnel and Payroll Information System (IPPIS), which was initiated by the Obasanjo Administration towards the end of his tenure. Through this technology we arranged for federal, civil and public servants to register their biometrics as a condition for receiving their salaries and as a result we weeded out over fifty thousand ghost workers and saved N15 billion every month which was then equivalent to $100 million.

In December 2014, attempts were made to divert monies meant for salaries and emoluments to some other Government expenditure. When that happened, the software which had its own defence mechanism shut the system down. Consequently, thousands of workers in some Ministries, Departments and Agencies (MDAs), could not get their December salaries paid early. They were eventually paid as soon as the anomaly was rectified. I apologised to those families who suffered but I believed that to fight corruption we had to take the necessary measures to establish and strengthen our institutions by adopting the best available technology. This is the only way to systematically and successfully fight corruption.

The effective implementation of these policies in 2014 brought positive results as Nigeria made its best improvement ever in Transparency International's (TI) Corruption Perception Index. Nigeria was ranked the 136th out of 175 nations surveyed; an improvement from the nation's previous position of 144th in 2013, 139th in 2012 and 143rd in 2011.

It is important to note that despite the many sensational stories, dramatic arrests, seizures and accusations, many of them false, since I left office, the fact remains that Nigeria has not made any improvement on TI Corruption Perception Index since 2014.

In fact, the 2017 corruption perception index released in 2018 by TI placed Nigeria as number 148, a retrogression in which the nation went 12 places backward. In other words, Nigeria is more corrupt in 2017 than it was when I handed over to the Buhari administration in 2015. Some people may be misled with smoke and mirrors but the TI Corruption Perception Index relies on unsentimental facts and figures.

Interestingly, just as I was about to end my work on this book, the Tribune, a newspaper founded by Chief Obafemi Awolowo, one of the founding fathers of independent Nigeria, of blessed memory, on the third year Democracy Day Anniversary of my successor, wrote a very interesting editorial. The newspaper, while coming down hard on all past leaders of Nigeria under the democratic dispensation, including me, said this about its perception of the anti-corruption fight and gave a verdict that corruption has worsened:

"...Nineteen years on, not only is the polity still afflicted by

worsening cases of poverty and corruption, the country's democratic credentials are virtually in tatters. Indeed, it is doubtful that democracy is being practised in the country, let alone being entrenched...."

One of the affirmations that my administration fought corruption also came from an unlikely source, Femi Falana, a Senior Advocate of Nigeria (SAN) and one of my unrelenting critics while speaking on TV affirmed that I fought corruption in my own way:

"Even President Goodluck Jonathan fought corruption in his own way. You will be surprised how he got results. For instance, last year, when the government had to withdraw the charges against Mr. Mohammed Abacha after 14 years, between year 2000 and 2014 that the case travelled between the FCT High Court to the Supreme Court. And when the government was now going to withdraw the charges at the High Court, because the Supreme Court said go back and have your trial, the Office of the Attorney General issued a statement to the effect that the withdrawal was occasioned by the fact that $970M from the Abacha loot has been recovered by the Jonathan's Government.

Under that Government, $458M was also forfeited by the United States Government which has not been repatriated yet; the United States Government, the Obama regime simply decided not to. This was from the Abacha loot alone. And from the Halliburton, from Siemen's scandal and some of them, through some plea-bargain, the Government made about $120M. That was the Jonathan Government! So, every government in Nigeria investigates the past, usually the previous regime but for the past 16 years, the PDP Government and the Abdulsalami Abubakar junta recovered about $3.2B from the Abacha loot. It is the most successful loot recovery in the world. And it has not ended yet; the Government's not done yet with the

Abacha loot alone. Again, to be fair to President Jonathan, he sacked three Ministers, one of them on the ground of conflict of interest for corruption..."

The accusation was made that my body language did not suggest I was willing to fight corruption. What some people wanted me to do was to go around the world announcing that Nigerians are corrupt. I believe that is not what a President should do. A President should fight corruption without stigmatizing its citizens. Yes, there are corrupt Nigerians but there are also many credible Nigerians at home and in the Diaspora. This is the case all over the world, albeit in varying degrees.

There are two options before us as a nation. We can continue to strengthen our institutions and plug the loopholes like my administration did and come up with reforms as I had earlier enumerated, or we keep parading a few individuals in handcuffs to feed the appetites of those who have entertained negative expectations while leaving intact the architecture of corruption.

Chapter Six

POWER STRUGGLE IN NIGERIA

"The beauty of democracy is that its practice is never final and always has room for improvement no matter how old a democratic society may be. Where we falter, we must not fall. When we are weak, we must not surrender"

Goodluck Ebele Jonathan
MARCH 29, 2010: NATIONWIDE BROADCAST TO MARK THE 2010 DEMOCRACY DAY IN ABUJA.

The population of Nigeria is said to have hit 198 million in 2018, based on projections by the National Population Commission (NPC) and this population is not uniformly distributed among the ethnic groups. Just like in most African countries, politics in Nigeria is tied to religion and ethnicity.

In most cases, the majority ethnic groups dominate the political landscape. This sparks and sustains tensions between the majority groups who want to maintain their dominance and the minorities who also want access to power as a means to show their relevance in the nation. Sometimes, when the domination by the majority is overbearing as to be emasculating, the minority goes to extreme lengths to resist which in many cases leads to calls for secession or civil wars.

Nigeria is a perfect example of the scenario I just painted. This is because of its unique plurality and huge population, its history, resources and placement in global consciousness and considerations. Everyone agrees that if Nigeria fell into a total all out fracas, it could mean an African apocalypse which would not just be difficult to contain but would certainly spill over to other nations of the world with disastrous impact. This is one of the reasons why it must not happen.

There are three major ethnic nationalities in Nigeria, with three distinct tongues, cultures and traditions. These are the Hausa/Fulani, Yoruba and Igbo. Actually there is nothing like Hausa/Fulani. You are either Hausa or Fulani, but popular mythology, especially in Southern Nigeria led to the emergence of the term Hausa/Fulani. These three ethnic nationalities are the tripod that dominates the political establishment in Nigeria. Political correctness would probably assail such an assertion but the truth is always difficult to ambush for long intervals.

Apart from these three dominant ethnic nationalities, there are at least 400 more with distinctly different languages and cultures too. If there was ever a single recipe for discord, none could possibly rival the ingenuity of Nigeria's chef. Yet, it has been managed since the country survived the civil war.

Since the Nigerian Civil War (1967-1970), these ethnic nationalities and their minority allies have managed their difficult marriage in such a way that political power flows in a predictable pattern.

As I stated earlier, my emergence as President did not follow the usual Nigerian trajectory to power. Although I am not by nature the most ambitious person, I insisted on running in 2011 to prove a point, which was that every Nigerian, irrespective of ethnicity or religion, should be able to aspire to the office of the Presidency once he or she is qualified. Today, the world has travelled much farther than the times when any agreements may have been reached to retain the Nigerian presidency amongst any privileged groups.

The power structure and political struggles of Nigeria dates back all the way to 1914. Before that date, the Northern and Southern parts of Nigeria were administered as two separate and independent protectorates under British colonial rule. The protectorates were amalgamated in January 1914 leading to the birth of present day Nigeria. Since then, and especially from independence in 1960, there has always been tension between the North and the South over who controls political power.

Let me give an insight into a background that has been violently ingrained into the minds of Nigerians since the nation came into being. Great Britain granted Nigeria her independence on the 1st of October, 1960. Sir Abubakar Tafawa Balewa was a Nigerian politician and the first and only Prime Minister of independent Nigeria. He played important roles in the country's early indigenous rule and was one of the African leaders in the formation of the Organization of African Unity (OAU), now the African Union (AU).

It is important to note that between independence on 1st of October 1960 and February 13, 1976, no Nigerian leader has had an orderly tenure. Every leader up to that point was either violently killed or violently overthrown.

This trend was bucked by Gen. Olusegun Obasanjo between 1976 and 1979. Unfortunately, the trend re-emerged after he handed over power and continued until the transitional regime of Gen. Abudulsalami Abubakar who handed over power to a democratically elected President produced by the PDP. The PDP has the singular honour of sustaining peaceful transitions and stability of the country for 16 years.

Here is a timeline of Nigerian leaders and how they quit the scene;

- Abubakar Tafawa Balewa, a Northern Muslim emerged as Prime Minister on the 1st of October 1960. On the 15th of January, 1966, he was overthrown and killed in a military coup. The coup and his death threw the North into outrage and turmoil. There were violent riots.

- After the death of Nigeria's first Prime Minister, Gen. Aguiyi-Ironsi, a Nigerian of Igbo stock, a Southern Christian succeeded Sir Tafawa Balewa and was also assassinated after 177 days in office on July 29, 1966.

- Gen. Yakubu Gowon, a Northern Christian from a minority ethnic group, took over after the assassination of Gen. Ironsi. He ruled for nine years and presided over the civil war. He was overthrown on the 29th of July, 1975.
- Gen. Murtala Mohammed, his successor, a Northern Muslim, was assassinated in a coup on the 13th of February, 1976 after six months in office.
- Gen. Olusegun Obasanjo, who was his second in command, succeeded him. He was a Christian Southerner of Yoruba stock and the first Nigerian ruler to have had an un-truncated regime. He restored civil rule on October 1, 1979 and handed over to President Shehu Shagari.
- Alhaji Shehu Shagari, a Northern Muslim, became the first civilian elected President. He was overthrown three months into his second term on the 31st of December, 1983.
- Major-General Muhammadu Buhari, a Northern Muslim succeeded President Shehu Shagari on the 31st of December 1983 and was overthrown 20 months into his government on the 27th of August, 1985.
- His successor, Gen. Ibrahim Babangida, a Northern Muslim, stepped aside after eight years as military Head of State, following the political impasse occasioned by the annulment of the June 12, 1993 elections believed to have been won by late Chief M.K.O Abiola, a Yoruba Southern Muslim.
- He was succeeded by Chief Ernest Shonekan, a Yoruba Southern Christian as head of the short-lived Interim National Government which was eased out by the military after 81 days on the 17th of November 1993.
- Gen. Sani Abacha, a Northern Muslim, who succeeded Shonekan, died in office after five years as military Head of State on the 8th of June, 1998.
- Gen. Abdusalam Abubakar, another Northern Muslim handed over power to a democratically elected President, Chief Olusegun Obasanjo on May 29th, 1999, nine months after he succeeded Abacha.
- Chief Olusegun Obasanjo who took over from Gen. Abubakar in 1999 spent two terms of four years each as a democratically elected President. His second term ended on May 29, 2007.
- Alhaji Umaru Musa Yar'Adua, a Northern Muslim, succeeded Obasanjo but died after three years in office on 5th May, 2010.
- As the Vice President and a Southern Christian minority, I took over

from late Yar'Adua to complete his tenure as enshrined in the constitution. Thereafter, I contested and won the 2011 Presidential election. My tenure ended on May 29, 2015. I was succeeded by President Muhammadu Buhari, former Military Head of State on May 29, 2015.

Now, from the above list, my readers will understand what I meant by emerging onto the scene as President against the established political order. Of the thirteen Heads of Government Nigeria has had, eight have been Hausa/Fulani (a majority ethnic nationality). Two of them have been Yoruba (another majority ethnic nationality). One of them was from a Northern ethnic minority and the other was Igbo (one of the three large majority tribes).

I remain the only one to be elected from a Southern minority ethnic nationality as President of Nigeria. My election was due to circumstances largely beyond human control. I became President against the established pattern of choosing Nigerian leaders from amongst the majority ethnicities.

Understanding the history of Nigeria and the attendant North-South political power play is crucial to appreciating the inner recesses of Nigeria's political dynamics. It would also allow you to easily follow my narrative with a clearer understanding when I begin to talk about elections, conflicts and how conspiracies, protests and schemings have become a way of political life in Nigeria.

My leadership was besieged by these contending primordial forces with the ever present threat of violence and intrigue. Lining the crevices of these forces are formidable modern players who, for mostly selfish reasons, were bent on not allowing these sentiments die a natural death.

Most of the intractable problems which bedevil governance in Nigeria proved endemic and enduring, not because they could not be easily solved or that the capacity to resolve them was absent, but because these problems were actually instituted and defended for tribal sentiments which address power points preferences.

It mattered crucially that I strayed into power coming from an ethnic group that is not considered one of the majority or aristocratic groups. It was worse in their consideration because I was also not individually blue-blooded. Perhaps it would have been less insulting to them if I had come from a wealthy background, but considering what the likes of Chief M.K.O Abiola went through despite his great wealth, it may not have mattered if I came from a moneyed background.

There is one way we could improve on this structure immediately and set everyone at ease. We either restructure or prepare ourselves for the inevitable. If we must rebuild Nigeria, it is beyond the responsibility of an individual or one political party.

Majority of Nigerians have obviously accepted the huge advantage derivable from the continued existence of this union and the frightening prospect of going into any kind of splinters. Nonetheless, there is a need for a fresh injection of political fidelity to the union; a reworking of the Federation such that minorities should not feel disadvantaged and marginalized.

To those who may want to ask why I did not do it when I had the chance, my response would be to ask them to study the 2014 National Conference report and what it was able to achieve. If the report is implemented, it will address most of the grey areas agitating the minds of Nigerians. Though I will touch on the National Conference report in later chapters, let me however quote from former Chief Justice Idris Kutigi, who chaired the Conference. He said: *"We have held a National Conference and we are more united today than ever."*

Chapter Seven

PRESIDENTIAL ELECTION CAMPAIGN

"I have come to launch a campaign of ideas, not one of calumny. I have come to preach love not hate. I have come to break you away from divisive tendencies of the past which has slowed down our drive to nationhood"

Goodluck Ebele Jonathan
SEPTEMBER 18, 2010: DECLARATION OF CANDIDACY
FOR THE PDP PRESIDENTIAL PRIMARIES

I ran for a second term expecting to win but knowing I could also lose. It was that possibility that would provide me the opportunity to show that my political philosophy was genuinely held and not just a campaign rhetoric.

The essence of my campaign was to promote democracy and social justice which encompasses love, peace and togetherness. I did not preach hate. Other political parties had other ideas and it was clear as soon as our campaign train entered the Northern part of Nigeria, especially the North West and North East which were the strongholds of my opponent. Young people were recruited to pelt my convoy with stones in three Northern States. The attack happened in Katsina on January 21, 2015, in Bauchi on January 22, 2015 and in Yola, Adamawa on January 29, 2015.

It is a treasonable offence to attack the convoy of a President. The security agents attached to me would have been justified if they had used deadly force, but I restrained them. Perhaps that is what those who instigated the attacks wanted. It was alarming that some older, highly placed people would use innocent children as cannon fodder, all for the sake of power. Such occurrences never happened in Southern Nigeria either to me or my main opponent.

On the days those youth were programmed to pelt my convoy with stones, the instigators were out for two things, the least of which was to embarrass their President. It was considered a huge mileage for their campaign. Humiliating the President of their country was fair game. At that point, they were not thinking of Nigeria, that is if they ever thought of Nigeria at all. The fury of their thirst for power did not allow them to think about the implications for the country.

They did not even think about the office they wanted and the consequences of diminishing it before it gets to them. It was single-minded recklessness. We could not but stare that history in the face.

The other thing they were out for and which they desperately hoped would happen, was for any of the youth to be wounded or even killed. It was a very tense situation. The Boko Haram menace was at its ugliest moments.

The Presidential security could easily have fired at the source of the missiles, thinking it was the insurgents. But we responded differently. I have always said it and meant it. Nothing I wanted was worth the blood of a human being, least of all, the people I had the direct charge to protect, the people I swore to serve.

Muhammadu Buhari was in my home State and I proactively ensured that nothing of that sort happened. He was not the President and it would have been easy to return the dubious compliment. There was no shortage of courageous young men ready to carry out such a mission. We could also have simply denied complicity as they did, but it was not my way. Besides not being so base by nature, I would have reduced an office I held in trust and embarrassed my colleagues and many others around the world who hold me to certain standards and values.

I encouraged my supporters not to dwell on the issue. When I accepted the PDP nomination for the re-elections, I had charged myself and my supporters to campaign in peace, with hope in our hearts, on the facts and truth, on issues and ideas, on our record of performance, not violence. Ours was a campaign of ideas.

We put it behind us and forged ahead with a clean campaign. The opposition was steeped in negative rhetoric and slurs of all manners. We were not swayed. I campaigned consistently on what we did, what we were doing and what we could still do. My concern was for new ideas and positive ways of doing things. It was important to purge the do or die mentality from our minds. It would take some time but I knew I was making head way in that direction. It showed by the huge drop in politically motivated assassinations. It simply vanished, because the leader was not interested in killing to win.

They raised a chorus of 'Jonathan must go'. They crafted a pseudo activist image. They loaded the campaign space with a lot of unproven corruption allegations. Whatever their mind could think of, their mouths readily expressed.

The propaganda exhibited by the opposition was infinitely worse than any one they could imagine and they imagined plenty. The point was to mislead the ordinary folks against the government. It was even taken to the ridiculous extent of claiming that I was behind Boko Haram. They said I planned it in order to reduce the number of northern voters.

A particular opposition politician, Nasir El-Rufai, who became the Governor of Kaduna State, went to the ridiculous extent of tweeting on August 9, 2014, that the then President of the Christian Association of Nigeria (CAN), Pastor Ayo Oritsejafor, and I were the sponsors of Boko Haram. He added that members of Boko Haram were not really Muslims but Christians disguised as Muslims for the purpose of spoiling Islam's good name. Of course, it was laughable and extremely ridiculous. On that same day, at the Portcullis House in Parliament, London, El-Rufai repeated the same allegations at an event.

The elections were scheduled for February 14, 2015 and all through the campaigns I was confident that we were going to win based on our performance as a government. We looked at the big picture and our areas of strength were evident. Where we appeared weak, we intensified efforts to address issues to increase our numbers. We were confident that victory was ours. We were sure of the states where we would certainly have a clear lead. We knew the states which we had a 50-50 chance and finally the states we would have the required 25% to satisfy the provisions of the law.

Obviously and with the benefit of hindsight, I have come to be aware of the intrigue that played a significant role in costing my party and I the election. For instance, there were Governors elected under the banner of my party, the Peoples Democratic Party, who did not wholeheartedly campaign for me and adamantly refused to allow campaign posters with my picture and theirs to be printed and circulated. In fact, a particular first term Governor in the North had openly said his ideal scenario was to have him re-elected and my opponent elected President. This same Governor told his aides that I would be removed in a coup. Unfortunately for him, his wishes did not come to pass and he ended up not being re-elected.

There was also a tremendous measure of religious pressure on members of the PDP from the North. This is not a fresh factor, but it is one militating against entrenching the ethos of democracy. For as long as people could be persuaded or harassed into falling in line by deploying religion as an instrument of politics, our goals for promoting democracy would prove difficult. I know that some would be eager to point at the American Evangelicals as a perfect example of religious mobilisation in an advanced democracy, but this would not invalidate our argument.

Although I do not believe that everything American is good to cite but in this instance, let me say that the American Evangelicals' role in elections is different from the role religion plays in Nigeria. No one forces or intimidates the Evangelicals to vote one way or the other. When elections are pre-determined by religion, we no longer practice true democracy. What we then have is some form of adulterated theocracy. Those religious sentiments stand in the way of performance, simply because you knew it only took your adherence to be approved. You therefore work towards your approval ratings amongst adherents of your religion rather than within the entire populace.

During the 2015 presidential elections campaigns, the opposition made unrealistic promises including monthly payout to all unemployed as well as creating millions of jobs annually, even without a clear picture of how the issue of capacity building would be adequately addressed. Those youth who innocuously built their hopes on these promises turned out to be the most disruptive during the elections because they erroneously saw any contrary position as one working against their destiny.

It was obvious that many of them did not have the capacity to understand that those promises were not supported by prevailing economic realities. My efforts in expanding the space for education, especially in building the Almajiri schools in the North were targeted at addressing those challenges. We have to continue to make deliberate effort to educate the Nigerian youth, particularly those in the Northern part of the country.

The Nigerian leadership must also embrace attitudinal change, not just rhetorical change. I believe that politics should be pursued with a reasonable degree of enlightenment and patriotism which requires honesty and transparency. Making fanciful promises falls out of line of these requirements. You would either be lying to a people you should be telling the whole truth or you lacked the capacity to figure out the status of your country's economy ahead of the possibility of your leadership.

I received information that some PDP leaders were alluding at this critical point to a breach of a spurious agreement as the reason for not supporting me. I was supposed to have entered the agreement before the 2011 elections. In Nigeria's political field, you could be in an agreement without knowing it and there usually was no need for documents validating such.

Let me however state without equivocation that I did not enter into any one term agreement with anybody. I have earlier challenged anyone who has contrary information or better still evidence, to publish it. The then Governor of Niger State, Dr. Muazu Babangida Aliyu is one of those who advocated the so called one term agreement. But I asked that if I had entered into a one term agreement with Governor Aliyu then, why did I lose the primary and general election in Niger State in 2011?

The enduring power struggle between North and South had taken on yet another life that significantly affected our poll numbers. We assessed the situation, re-strategized and adjusted our campaign. Within the PDP, some members from the North worked for the opposition not necessarily because of convictions or principles. The dissension had the effect of a rapid spread. Voters were clearly told not to vote for PDP in the Presidential election but were allowed to exercise their discretion in the choice of candidates for other elections. Some of those who engineered these scenarios were PDP members who were State Governors and some occupied offices in my Government.

It will be tough to trust this brood of politicians going forward, but we must not allow such thoughts to rubbish a stable and trustworthy relationship between North and South. I believe it is the political structure that must change in order to cure ourselves of this distrust.

Rescheduling of Elections

I distinctly remember receiving calls suggesting a rescheduling of the elections because weeks before, an average of 35% to 50% of the voters, depending on which part of the country they were located, had not received their permanent voters cards (PVC). There were several concerns raised in the public space about attempts to influence the electoral process. While this went on, the National Security Adviser stated that the military could not guarantee security in parts of the North-East, especially in Borno, Yobe, Gombe and Adamawa States.

The media was awash with Governors leading protests in their States. Almost all the Governors of the Southern States were shouting themselves hoarse, because of the low rates of PVC collection in the South.

A short while before the elections were rescheduled, Boko Haram militants had taken hold of a large cache of military grade weaponry, including Armoured Personnel Carriers from retreating Nigerian troops.

I requested an update from security officials who confirmed my fears. The group had almost five thousand fighters behind its growing effort to carve out an Islamic caliphate in the North Eastern geopolitical zone of Nigeria, around Cameroon, Chad and Niger Republic borders. Tension was thus further inflamed.

The opposition party, my critics and some Nigerians in the diaspora pressed for the elections to go on as scheduled. They had a different but unrealistic view of the situation. They were focused on just the elections, but you had to have a country after elections. It was my duty to keep the country intact after my service and I was not going to let the country go into crises that could even lead to disintegration.

It was worse for them because they saw mischief in every move our government made. Indeed there was no basis for the sightings of these constant apparitions because my administration was one that was pointedly devoid of treachery. However, I suppose the elections were more important to them than the lives we could have lost in the North-East if we had not taken charge and made the correct decision.

There were opinions that the NSA should not have broken the news about the possible rescheduling of the election abroad. I still wonder what difference the location of the announcement would have made in a global village, but such was the spirit of those times. They even alleged that I was about to launch a tenure elongation agenda. Nothing in my nature lent credence to such accusation. Prior to 2015, my party had lost quite a number of important elections and my posture did not switch from one of adherence to democracy.

I think the opposition was reacting to its own imagination. There were very concrete reasons to reshedule the election, even for a longer period as long as the handover date remained sacrosanct. We took the time we needed and did not postpone for a second longer. In any case, the accusation of tenure elongation was meaningless since I still had a term left under the constitution. I can recall that President Obama sent his Secretary of State to Nigeria, a sovereign nation, to protest the rescheduling of the election. John Kerry arrived in Nigeria on Sunday January 25, 2015 and said *inter alia "It's imperative that these elections happen on time as scheduled."*

Nigeria's leading online newspaper, Premium Times, reported Kerry's visit of January 25, 2015, as follows:

> "United States Secretary of State, John Kerry, is expected in Nigeria ahead of the country's general election, an agency report has indicated. According to Associated Press, AP,
>
> Mr. Kerry will make a stop-over in Lagos on Sunday to meet with President Goodluck Jonathan and Muhammadu Buhari, Presidential candidates of the Peoples Democratic Party, PDP, and the All Progressives Congress, APC, respectively....
>
> "Mr. Kerry's brief visit is a departure from the U.S. policy that disallow its senior officials from visiting countries about to hold elections, to avoid the perception of supporting one candidate against another. This is the first time a chief American diplomat is visiting the country since 2012...."

How can the US Secretary of State know what is more important for Nigeria than Nigeria's own government? How could they have expected us to conduct elections when Boko Haram controlled part of the North East and were killing and maiming Nigerians? Not even the assurance of the sanctity of the May 29, 2015 handover date could calm them down. In Nigeria, the constitution is very clear. No President can extend his tenure by one day.

On March 23, 2015, President Obama himself took the unusual step of releasing a video message directly to Nigerians all but telling them how to vote. In that video, Obama urged Nigerians to open the "next chapter" by their votes. Those who understood subliminal language deciphered that he was prodding the electorate to vote for the opposition to form a new government. The message was so condescending, it was as if Nigerians did not know what to do and needed an Obama to direct them.

In his message he said "all Nigerians must be able to cast their votes without intimidation or fear," yet his government was vehemently and publicly against the postponement of the elections to enable our military defeat Boko Haram and prevent them from intimidating voters. This was the height of hypocrisy!

The decision and announcement to postpone the elections was eventually made by the only body which could do so under the constitution. I should talk briefly about the INEC here because of the insinuations that my administration muscled INEC to make the pronouncement. Of course, nothing could be farther from the truth as people came to realize. Yes, the posture of INEC could appear edgy, but it knew it was not ready and that the election was too important to mess up.

The PVC shortage was everywhere. The lopsided collection of PVC caused an uproar that grew into a national din. The suspected housing of PVCs in the custody of non-INEC personnel was an issue. There were also issues with card readers. All of these happening despite years of preparation and substantial funds made available. It was all building up to a perfect storm, but those were INEC's problems which we were willing to help resolve.

Even then, the security of our country was our job and the military advised as they deemed fit. Before the election was eventually rescheduled by INEC, I summoned all the Service Chiefs, the NSA, Inspector General of Police (IGP), Director General of Directorate of State Security (DGDSS), among others to get further information. Then I called a meeting of the Council of State and requested the heads of security services and the INEC chairman to attend. These were not apolitical, but at least they could rise above politics and represent the interest of the entire country. At the end of deliberations, it was agreed that the elections be postponed for six weeks in order to create a safer environment for voters and officials on Election Day.

Let me add that the Council of State comprises all former Presidents and Heads of State, all former Chief Justices of the Federation and all the 36 serving State Governors who are from different political parties.

The INEC was then directed to hold meetings with political parties while the NSA was to brief them on the security angle to the rescheduling. The vote in favour of the rescheduling was overwhelming. INEC thereafter announced the rescheduling of the election to the nation. I must add that beyond security concerns, one finds it difficult to understand how INEC or the political parties would want elections held at a time when more than 30% of the Nigerian electorates were yet to get their PVCs. This would have disenfranchised a significant portion of the electorates.

The foreign pressure on the issue of election rescheduling was intense. They maintained the curious posture of one who had been deceived before and therefore had every reason to cede no credence to our position. But there was no reason to have such a posture.

The United States and the United Kingdom were especially agitated. David Cameron, then the U.K. Prime Minister, called to express his concern about the election rescheduling, just as John Kerry came from the United States to express further worry. It was at best unusual and sobering. In fact, John Kerry did not accept our reasons for the rescheduling.

It was unbelieveable because at the back of our minds we knew why the agitation was beyond what meets the eyes. There were deeper political interests.

In attendance at the meeting of the Council of State where the decision to reschedule the election was taken were almost all the living former Heads of State of this country. That should have convinced John Kerry of the good intentions of the government. He cannot claim to love and defend Nigeria more than all our former heads of state present at the meeting. I have stated earlier how Kerry's visit was designed to humiliate a sitting Nigerian president and clearly take sides in the country's election.

Anyhow, the six weeks served us well. We received the military equipment we were expecting within that period and our Armed Forces commendably dealt a deserving blow on the terrorists and repossessed all territorial areas of Nigeria previously occupied by the terrorists. Boko Haram was deflated up to the point I handed over to my successor on May 29, 2015.

We conducted the elections peacefully, even if there were issues raised about its fairness. At least, the nation was relieved that the election held peacefully and that there was no post-election violence.

Chapter Eight

PRESIDENTIAL ELECTION

"Our determination and insistence on credible elections is now a movement whose final destination is electoral justice"

Goodluck Ebele Jonathan
MARCH 16, 2010: AT THE OPENING OF A THREE-DAY NATIONAL CONFERENCE FOR STAKEHOLDERS IN THE ELECTORAL PROCESS

The previous six weeks had been the longest of my life and the climax finally came that cool morning of the 28th of March, 2015, the Presidential Election Day. Sceptics and mischief makers had flown the non-existent kite of tenure elongation, interim government and all the other shenanigans they could come up with to blackmail my administration and make us look bad in the eyes of Nigerians and the international community.

As is customary, I flew to my community, Otuoke in my State, Bayelsa, to cast my ballot. Some hours into the election I received some disturbing signals. INEC officials in Southern Nigeria were insisting on the use of card readers while in the Northern part of the country, the decision to use card reader had been de-emphasized. It was clear that something was wrong somewhere. Tension was brewing in the country because the card readers were malfunctioning.

The intelligence report I had received also carried the spectre of the fabled American intelligence community prediction about the collapse of the Nigerian nation state. The disintegration of Nigeria was a possibility if I contested the results of the election, no matter how justified. There were justifiable grounds but I was determined that Nigeria will not disintegrate during my tenure.

The fate of thousands of Christians and Southerners in the North and my other Northern supporters, who were at the risk of being slaughtered if I took a selfish decision, lay heavily on my mind. Reprisals were certain to follow in the South. What rang persistently in my mind was the futility of vanity. What would it profit me if I clung on to power and let my country slide into an avoidable crisis? Who would stop the impending crisis? Too many things were bound to go wrong!

The multiple massacres which characterized the aftermath of the 2011 elections were still fresh in my memory. I was neither willing nor ready to look grieving children and parents in the eye and explain to them that they lost their loved ones because of leadership struggle. Already some Nigerian citizens and external forces had plans that were not good for our country.

I had every reason to contest the results, starting from educational qualification for elections and electoral malpractices. These were the facts in my hands, but there was also the question of worth. Was it worth it? I reflected on some details. My country had been under colonial rule and our fathers mounted a struggle for freedom from the colonial masters. Without shedding blood, we gained our independence. How could I now be party to a decision that would result in rivers of blood which would flow across the land?

I thought deeply about the hand it had pleased God to deal me. My rise to the pinnacle of power in a country of 180 Million people (in 2010), most of whom would give anything to be where I had been, was already cause for eternal gratitude.

I thought about the economy to which we dedicated long hours and hard labour which had only recently officially become the largest economy in Africa. Every three months, I had chaired the meetings of the Economic Management Team involving the top players of the organised private sector and key government officials. Those meetings of the economic management team usually lasted upwards of three hours. How could I jeopardise all our joint efforts?

I thought about the policies my administration had put in place just to convince genuine foreign investors to invest in Nigeria. I imagined all those huge investments simply coming to ruins. Could I sincerely let all those investments go to waste? We toiled to make the Nigerian economy the number one destination for foreign investment in Africa, as published in the World Investment Report of the United Nations Conference on Trade and Development (UNCTAD), 2013. Could I then watch the destruction of that same economy?

In my capacity as Nigeria's President, I worked with other Presidents to resolve the political crises in some West African countries. In Cote d'Ivoire alone, thousands of human beings were killed in post-election violence. There were other crises in the sub-region which we helped resolve. How would I discuss Nigeria's stability with my colleagues from ECOWAS? What do I tell them?

From 1967 to 1970, Nigeria fought a very bitter civil war in which millions of lives were lost. That war was fought over a secession attempt by a region which was the culmination of unsettled issues stemming from the disputed 1965 Western Region of Nigeria election which eventually led to the first military coup in Nigeria on 15 January 1966. The consequences of the civil war are still haunting us till date. Did I want history to repeat itself? Could I partake in the reincarnation of that war which sent hundreds of thousands of Nigerians to an early grave? A war which razed down my own very community? From the interim report before me, youth had been armed and mobilized to unleash mayhem. Provisions of guns, petrol bombs, knives and other incendiary substances had been made in full readiness for maelstrom on a massive scale.

This was not surprising giving the threat by the main opposition party, to form a parallel government if the elections were "rigged". Every election that had not been won by the opposition in the past was considered rigged.

An eerie comment was made two years before by the then main opposition candidate, threatening that "if what happened in 2011 should again happen in 2015, by the grace of God, the dog and the baboon would all be soaked in blood."

Of course what happened in 2011 is that the opposition had lost the Presidential election that was unanimously adjudged free and fair by both international and local observer missions. The former Botswanan President, Festus Mogae, who led the Commonwealth Election Observer Group, returned the following verdict, describing the election to be "orderly and transparent and therefore a pleasant surprise given the fact that this country has been notorious for flawed elections." Mr. Mogae, said further he was "very impressed" by the election stressing that other observers had adjudged it the most credible election since Nigeria returned to civil rule in 1999.

When I met with then President Obama after the 2011 elections, he told me that from the information they had, the elections were free and fair. Yet, here was the opposition threatening to "soak" the country in blood if the same thing occurred in 2015. Indeed when my opponent challenged the results of the 2011 elections in the Court of Appeal, all five Justices unanimously upheld the results of the election. The same happened at the Supreme Court where all seven Justices again unanimously upheld the results of the election. There was no minority judgment in both appellate courts.

As I said earlier, recalling 2011 was too easy. I won the election but the nation lost many lives. Youth were mobilized to cause havoc in the North despite the fact that there were no genuine disputes about my victory. That victory ended up tasting like ash in my mouth because of the loss of lives and mindless destruction of properties. The murders were as many as they were foul; properties worth billions of naira of many Nigerians in the North perceived to have sympathy for me were destroyed.

By the time the 2015 elections came, it was practically impossible for my supporters in some parts of the North to go out and canvass for me; and in fact, on election day, to go out and vote. Threats of violence against them were palpable and real. This was particularly so because of the bitter experience of the 2011 elections in which more than 500 people in Kaduna were killed including the brutal murder of the 10 NYSC members in Bauchi in the aftermath of the declaration of the elections.

The fact that I got only 16% of the votes in Bauchi State was an indication that the reasons for the killings went beyond the results of the election from the State.

The alleged sin of those NYSC members was serving their fatherland as INEC ad hoc staff on Election Day. It had since stuck to my memory. Hundreds of thoughts flashed through my mind in each round of reflection. Could we ever play politics without bitterness in this country? The phrase raised the image of one of our great leaders in my mind, late Alhaji Waziri Ibrahim. His advocacy was "politics without bitterness."

Alhaji Waziri Ibrahim, the leader of the defunct Great Nigeria People's Party (GNPP), during the Second Republic had preached on why bitterness must not be a permanent component of Nigeria's politics. When he looked at the results of the 1979 elections, he described it as "super rigging". Alhaji Waziri was unhappy but never bitter.

Nigeria was at the brink of a major explosion. Many who could afford airline tickets had already sent or were planning to send their families overseas. Those who could not afford to leave the country were sending their loved ones to neighbouring nations, or their villages and towns. The flight from this unseen but impending catastrophe was happening more in the big cities like Lagos, Abuja, Kano and Katsina.

I felt so sad for the youth prepped to kill and destroy. I was apprehensive of human lives that would be lost, properties and investments worth trillions of naira going up in flames. I had genuine fears that my country would no longer be one if I took to serve my personal interest.

It was at this point that the breakthrough came to me as something in my spirit recalled the single phrase I was noted for saying, 'my ambition is not worth the blood of any Nigerian!' This was my mantra when I ran for election into the office of the Governor of Bayelsa State in 2006 and it gained a prominent echo during my Presidential campaign in 2011 and 2015.

I knew instantly that if I clung on to power, latching on to some of the identified infractions of the elections, there was a possibility that Nigeria may have imploded. If it was just that perhaps some people may have been pleased but it was not just that Nigeria's corporate existence would be threatened, it would have first been "soaked in blood."

I had worked hard to consolidate and protect the independence of INEC that conducted an acceptable election in 2011. Can I tell the world that the same INEC had changed because of some interest? It was a burden for me as a sitting President to tell the world that the same INEC had performed differently in the 2015 elections.

The division along religions and ethnic lines was sharp. The positions were firm and decided. It was a very dangerous moment which could not be taken for granted. The prediction of the U.S intelligence community on the disintegration of Nigeria was an additional concern. Such intelligence is not to be ignored. Not that all their predictions come to pass but indicators pointed to a great likelihood that this one may have been a correct call.

The spill over scenario of Nigeria's population throughout the West African and Central African sub-regions was always the nightmare of Heads of Government and everybody involved in the vigil for peace in the region and far beyond. I refused to bear that burden. I knew I had to act swiftly.

The Presidential Election Results

I knew what was coming the day before I called General Muhammadu Buhari. I had reports on the polls around the country. It was clear the results were not going to favour me. Apparently, there were many instances of irregularities. There were series of problems with card readers, resulting from widespread technical hitches leading to the non-uniform application throughout the country.

For some inexplicable reason, the INEC had been able to achieve near 100% distribution of Permanent Voter Cards in the North, including the North East, which was under siege with the Boko Haram insurgency but failed to record a similar level of distribution in the South which was relatively more peaceful.

Social media was filled with all manner of stories, pictures and videos. I was settled in my mind that I was not going to be the sitting President pointing out these infractions and accusing the opposition and the very INEC I helped to strengthen.

The world saw my ordeal at the polling unit in my community in Bayelsa State, where the card reader refused my PVC even after we tried repeatedly during acreditation. And it was the same with my wife and my mother. It was a moment that exposed the shortcomings of INEC.

However, I was heading towards peace. Stopping the election on voting day would have been like detonating an atomic bomb. After we managed to vote upon filling the Incident Forms, I left Bayelsa for Abuja to monitor the elections and collation of results all over the country from the 29th to 31st March, 2015.

The country was tense. I had to do something. I could no longer wait for the collation of the final results. The pressure on the country was palpable. In Lagos, people were ready to burst loose on the streets and in the North; the stage was set for envisaged violence. One of my party's agents at the INEC National Collation Centre in Abuja, Elder Godsday Orubebe eventually got into a heated argument with the INEC Chairman, Prof. Attahiru Jega. That further raised the tension in the country. Everyone was expecting the worst. I knew it was time to douse the tension.

As I said earlier, I was fully informed about the manipulations, intrigues, intimidations and betrayals. The consequences of not conceding were only better imagined. My natural instinct for peace automatically surfaced. I was going to make a decision which reflected my commitment to that ideal. This is the foundation of my essence. In my periodic projections into the future, I did not see how I would be presiding over any kind of chaos. I was prepared to promote the peace, unity and progress of Nigeria.

This is a huge sacrifice, but I hope my readers believe me when I say it turned out to be one of the easiest decisions I ever took while in office. With my mind made up, I knew it was time to inject peace into the tense polity, especially before INEC completed collation.

I was in my living room with some Ministers, aides and friends. Among them were the Coordinating Minister for the Economy/Honourable Minister of Finance, Dr. Mrs. Ngozi Okonjo-Iweala, Honourable Attorney General of the Federation and Minister of Justice, Mohammed Bello Adoke, SAN, the Honourable Minister of Aviation, Mr. Osita Chidoka and Waripamowei Dudafa, my Senior Special Assistant on Domestic Affairs.

They were recommending sundry alternatives, but I was quiet in the midst of their discussion. I hugged my thoughts, figuring out how to do that which was best for the country. My personal interest was receding rapidly and the interest of Nigeria looming large. I excused myself and left the sitting room. I walked into my study. Even here, my mantra was a strong circle around me, supporting and comforting me. Let the country survive. Let democracy survive. My political ambition is not worth people being 'soaked in blood'.

More reports flowed in and I could not wait anymore. The announcement of the final result could take issues out of all our hands. It was time for me to take action and bring peace to the nation. I felt I was destined by God at that point in time to inject the peace serum and douse the palpable tension in the country.

I reached for the telephone and placed a call through the State House operators at about 4:45 pm. A peace I had never felt since my political sojourn, descended on me. It showed me where I had been in the past sixteen years and where I was then. I smiled at the thought of what I was about to do. I waited calmly for the person at the other end of my call to answer.

Buhari: "Hello Your Excellency!"
Me: "Your Excellency, how are you?"
Buhari: "I am alright Your Excellency"
Me: "Congratulations!"
Buhari: "Thank you very much Your Excellency..."

For several seconds the line was seized by the loudest silence I have ever known. Then we had a brief discussion. I could sense his relief too. He knew what could have been. Here is a man who had contested three times and lost. Maybe my gesture humbled him against his expectations because he thanked me and we talked about the handing over processes.

Everywhere all over Africa, Asia and other parts of the world, countless deaths have been recorded on the scores of elections and power disputes. I mentioned Cote d'Ivoire earlier, where people died in their thousands during post-election violence. A similar scenario had unfolded in Kenya. African nations are more prone to post-election violence than other parts of the world. Only very few African nations have not experienced post-elections violence on a very grand scale or some bitter power tussle fed by tribal or ethnic sentiments.

I hung up the phone, confident that my decision was right for Nigeria and would probably have a great impact on Africa. This may well be the beginning of a new perspective to power; a perspective which places national interest above personal preference. It should not always be about winning.

After my conversation with Muhammadu Buhari, which lifted my spirit greatly, I felt better and lighter; it was time to break the news to my Ministers and aides. I wandered back into the living room. These are people I came to know over a period of time. I anticipated what their response would be.

In my new found calm, I stood before them and told them what I had just done. The elections were over. I had called and congratulated Muhammadu Buhari on his victory. It was time for all of us to move on. Stunned silence greeted the room for some time and after they overcame their shock, they all congratulated me.

My Aviation Minister, Osita Chidoka, sought my permission to tweet my phone conversation with Muhammadu Buhari. I obliged and he did. The country was no longer waiting for the declaration of the election results. The nationwide tension automatically dissipated as though a red hot piece of iron had been dipped in a bowl of water.

Thereafter I addressed the nation:

> *Fellow Nigerians,*
>
> *I thank you all for turning out en-masse for the March 28 General Elections. I promised the country free and fair elections. I have kept my word. I have also expanded the space for Nigerians to participate in the democratic process. That is one legacy I will like to see endure. Although some people have expressed mixed feelings about the results announced by the Independent National Electoral Commission (INEC), I urge those who may feel aggrieved to follow due process based on our constitution and our electoral laws, in seeking redress. As I have always affirmed, nobody's ambition is worth the blood of any Nigerian. The unity, stability and progress of our dear country are more important than anything else.*
>
> *I congratulate all Nigerians for successfully going through the process of the March 28th General Elections with the commendable enthusiasm and commitment that was demonstrated nationwide. I also commend the Security Services for their role in ensuring that the elections were mostly peaceful and violence-free.*
>
> *For my colleagues in the PDP, I thank you for your support. Today, the PDP should be celebrating rather than mourning. We have established a legacy of democratic freedom, transparency and economic growth. For the past sixteen years, we have steered the country away from ethnic and regional politics. We created a Pan-Nigerian political party and brought*

home to our people the realities of economic development and social transformation. Through patriotism and diligence, we have built the biggest and most patriotic party in Nigeria history.

We must stand together as a party and look to the future with renewed optimism. I thank all Nigerians once again for the great opportunity I was given to lead this country and assure you that I will continue to do my best at the helm of national affairs until the end of my tenure.

I have conveyed my personal best wishes to General Muhammadu Buhari. May God almighty continue to bless the Federal Republic of Nigeria.

I thank you all.

On that day, history was made. There have been attempts to rewrite that history with different accounts as to why and how I conceded defeat to Muhammadu Buhari. Some are totally false while some are only half-truths. The unkindest cut of them all was made by Professor John Paden in his book, 'Muhammadu Buhari: *The Challenges of Leadership in Nigeria*', where he falsely alleged, that I was pressured by foreign leaders to concede. On page 68 of the book, Paden said: "*There was considerable international pressure on Jonathan, which included the Archbishop of Canterbury and Western Diplomats.*"

The above quotation is clearly fabricated because rather than foreign leaders calling to put pressure on me to concede, the reality was that they called to congratulate me after I had conceded. How could anyone have pressured me when the Electoral Commission was still collating the results as at the time I called to congratulate Muhammadu Buhari. Professor Paden's account is obviously a deliberate falsehood.

Chapter Nine

THE WORLD RESPONDS

"As the most populous black nation on earth, it seemed our manifest destiny, is to champion the cause of African emancipation and integration"

Goodluck Ebele Jonathan
AUGUST 1, 2011: AT A RETREAT TO REVIEW THE NATION'S FOREIGN POLICY

In the weeks following my decision to concede, there was a gale of messages acknowledging what I had done and congratulating me from all over the world. It was commended as a giant step in avoiding violence, genocide and untold hardships in the land. I was pleasantly surprised that Nigerians and foreigners saw my decision as historic. The calls were streaming in and so were the letters, especially from the West African leaders who all wrote personal letters to me. One of the letters in particular came from the President of the Economic Community of West African States (ECOWAS).

They knew I had always been on the forefront of negotiations for peace in the ECOWAS sub-region. They knew if I had decided to play the power game instead of conceding, the entire region would have been submerged under a deluge of refugees.

At the 47th Ordinary Session of the Authority in Accra on May 19, 2015, the President of the Republic of Ghana, who was also the Chairman of the Authority of Heads of State and Government of ECOWAS, Mr. John Mahama, during his opening address, led other leaders to show their appreciation. He noted that the success of the Nigerian election as well as that of Togo had sent a strong message to the world that the ECOWAS protocol on democracy and good governance was working.

Furthermore, his speech read:

> *"Let me on your behalf take this opportunity to highly commend our brother, President Goodluck Jonathan for his personal show of mature statesmanship in the event that followed the Presidential election held in Nigeria. I believe his name will be recorded in a special place when the history of Nigeria's democracy comes to be written."*

In a message he gave at that session, the then Secretary General of the UN, Mr. Ban Ki-Moon, praised me for my contributions to regional peace and security. He was represented by his special representative for ECOWAS,

Ambassador Muhammed Ibn Chambas, who said:

> *"As this marks the final summit of President Goodluck Jonathan, I wish to send our sincere appreciation for his valuable contributions to regional integration, maintenance of peace and security in West Africa, most notably In Cote d'ivoire, Guinea and Mali."*

In his address, the president of the ECOWAS Commission, Kadré Désiré Ouedraogo acknowledged the credibility Nigeria had brought to ECOWAS with the 2015 elections.

He said the commission would never forget my contributions to the management and resolution of crisis in West Africa. He further said:

> *"In that respect, I think firstly of the increased credibility that ECOWAS has received due to the conduct of the Presidential election in Nigeria and the manner in which it was concluded."*

Speaking particularly to me, he said:

> *"I wish to assure him that the commission will never forget his crucial contribution in the management and resolution of crisis in Guinea Bissau, Mali and Burkina Faso as well as in the fight against the Ebola virus disease among other challenging matters. I am confident that nothing will come to make us forget the great pride Nigeria has brought us only a few*

President Goodluck with ECOWAS Heads of States and Government at his valedictory Summit in Accra, Ghana, May 19th 2015

Here is the full text of my valedictory speech as Nigeria's leader at that ECOWAS summit:

Mr. Chairman,

I must start this brief remark by expressing my profound appreciation to you, the Government and people of Ghana for the warm reception accorded me and my delegation since my arrival here in Accra. The traditional warm hospitality that has been extended inspires admiration of the brotherly people of Ghana. It also certainly underscores the committed, forthright and exemplary leadership that you have personally offered our sub-region since assuming the chairmanship of the ECOWAS Authority of Heads of State and Government.

Similarly, may I also thank the President of ECOWAS commission for the earnest efforts that went into the convening of this 47th ordinary summit of ECOWAS. It is no wonder that our Organization continues to move from strength to strength in the face of both the strong leadership provided by our Chairman and the tireless work of the commission under its President and staff.

As we are all aware, this summit coincides with the 40th anniversary of the establishment of our Organization. I believe that this milestone calls for acknowledgment of the exceptional vision of the founding fathers which has inspired a united approach to addressing our common challenges. Unity of purpose and action has enabled us to build our strength as we move forward to enhanced sub-regional cooperation and integration. The significant progress we have made so far can only be sustained and built upon through even closer consultations, collaboration and cohesion amongst us.

With regard to our integration agenda, it must be said that we have achieved considerable progress. We have gone beyond our protocol on Free Movement of Persons and Goods, to the harmonization of trade and our customs codes. The achievement of the ECOWAS Common External Tariff and Trade Liberalization Scheme, are vital sign posts in the Convergence Criteria required for our common currency regime.

In our resolve to further enhance trade and facilitate transportation, work is in progress on the construction of the Lagos-Abidjan highway which would be completed by the formation of the Joint Border Posts Reconstruction Projects across our borders. In the last few months, for instance, President Boni Yayi and I were able to lay the foundation stone of the Joint Border Post between our two countries at Seme Border. My country, Nigeria, remains fully committed to the goal of an integrated and single West African community of nations and people. We have, therefore, spared no efforts in ensuring the early detection of conflict and in taking necessary measures for its elimination in our sub region. We do so on the strong conviction that without peace, there would be no development; and that our peoples cannot be weaned out of poverty and deprivation without development.

I have profound satisfaction and pride, especially when I see the remarkable progress that we have achieved together for our sub region. Our exertions in the quest for solutions to the political and security challenges that occasionally threaten the peace and stability of our nations is the hallmark of our common resolve to achieve our integration agenda. Indeed, our outstanding record on this score remains a model for all of Africa's other sub-regional Organisations.

I recall that as acting President, I became the Chairman of ECOWAS in 2010. This was a unique honour from my colleagues for which I remain grateful. The first challenge that we confronted was the situation in Niger Republic. Happily, through dogged efforts on our part, we were able to resolve it and the country returned to democratic rule. General Salou Djibo who oversaw the return to constitutional rule in Niger Republic is today a student at Ahmadu Bello University in Zaria, Nigeria.

In Cote d'Ivoire, ECOWAS followed through in its commitment to enduring democracy by standing firm behind the winner of the Presidential Elections in 2010. We are pleased that our brother, President Alassane Ouattara took his rightful place and went on not only to provide leadership to his country, but also as chairman of ECOWAS. Similarly, in both Guinea and Guinea Bissau, we remained focused on the goal of ensuring that viable political solutions were found for the political and security challenges that they were experiencing. That peace and stability and democratic governance have returned to these brotherly countries underscore our commitment to finding viable solutions to the problems of our sub-region.

As co-mediator, I visited Mali and met with all the stakeholders in early and difficult times of the crisis in the efforts towards return to democratic rule, maintenance of peace and articulation of viable political process. Nigeria participated in all the negotiations and meetings coordinated by ECOWAS at various venues that eventually produced a political time table for the holding of democratic elections in Mali.

Therefore, let me take this opportunity to felicitate with our brother, President Ibrahim Boubacar Keita, the Government and people of Mali for the historic peace and reconciliation Agreement signed in Bamako on 15th May, 2015, by all parties. It is our hope that this accord will signal the end of the Malian crisis.

With respect to the situation in Burkina Faso, fully aware of the serious consequence for stability in the region, our chairman, President Mahama, President Sall and I paid a consultative visit to Burkina Faso to engage on a plan of action to return the country to constitutionality. This initial engagement was subsequently followed-up by necessary ECOWAS mechanisms which assisted in calming the then tense political situation. I, therefore, urge that the stakeholders stay firm on the political roadmap that has been agreed by all parties.

Your Excellencies, the consolidation of democracy, the elevation of the rule of law and the deepening culture of good governance across our sub-region today, is the product of our solidarity and the growing effectiveness and integrity of the institutions and mechanisms that we have put in place. The elections in Ghana and Senegal were largely peaceful on their own without controversy and indicate a maturation of democracy in our sub-region. Equally, in Benin, Sierra Leone and now in Togo, we have made tremendous progress in consolidating democracy in our sub-region.

Permit me therefore, to congratulate my brother, His Excellency, Faure Essozimna Gnassingbe, on his recent re-election as President of the Republic of Togo. The successful conduct of that election devoid of violence and held in a free, fair and credible manner further confirms that democracy has indeed come to stay in our sub-region. We look forward to the same happy and tranquil outcome in all the member states where elections will also take place later in the year and subsequently.

Your Excellencies, while we are making progress in many core areas, there are issues that require our attention. In the past few years, we have witnessed a growing wave of young men and women from our sub-region undertaking very perilous journeys across the Sahara Desert and Mediterranean Sea to Europe. The phenomenon, given its hazardous nature, has claimed many lives and assumed humanitarian crisis. ECOWAS in the first instance should earnestly address this problem. I also urge that this matter be tabled at the forthcoming 24th summit of the African Union in June in South Africa. At the level of member states, we should take necessary action to address the root causes of the crisis.

Occasionally, our decision-making mechanisms which should, naturally, inform our consensual positions on matter that touch on our collective and sub-regional interest is not always upheld. Occasionally, our solidarity seems to face severe tests in the face of individual discretions and critical issues. I recall here our disparate positions and actions at crucial moments on the crisis in Cote d'Ivoire in 2011, and also, the choice of a candidate for the post of President of the Africa Union in 2012.

Again, at our last session in Abuja it was resolved, after due deliberations, that ECOWAS should adopt a single candidate for the post of President of the African Development Bank (AfDB). Today, we have no less than four candidates from our sub-region alone vying for the post as against four candidates representing the other four regions of the continent. Our experience with the Economic Partnership Agreement (EPA) with the European Union (EU) is yet another example. This recurring disposition elicits negative signals from our partners and other regions of the continent. It goes against the grain of the solidarity we all too often display in dealing with other challenges. We must rise above it in the larger interest of our sub-region.

Your Excellencies, as you are no doubt aware, this is the last summit that I will be attending as the president of the Federal Republic of Nigeria. In 10 days time, precisely on the 29th of this month, my successor, President-elect, General Muhammadu Buhari, will assume the mantle of leadership in my country. I feel deeply satisfied that the tree of democracy planted in my country and in our sub-region, has taken roots and its blossoming. I have no doubt whatsoever, that under the watchful guidance and nurturing of your Excellencies, that tree will continue to bear abundant fruits. Let me, therefore, seize the opportunity to express my profound appreciation for the understanding and cooperation that you accorded me all these years, especially during my tenure as the Chairman of our Organization between 2010-2012.

The personal rapport and chemistry that I have enjoyed with each one of you, my brother and sister Presidents greatly facilitated the decisions that we are able to take and the concrete measures we took on behalf of our sub-region. As the new Administration takes over, I am confident that the bonds of friendship between Nigeria and each member state of our cherished Organization and Nigeria's role within ECOWAS will grow even stronger. I urge you all to extend the same friendship and fraternal cooperation that I have received from you to my successor.

Once again, your Excellencies, I thank you for your friendship and the unalloyed support. I wish you well as you steer the affairs of our sub-region. The future of our organization and West Africa is in good, safe and capable hands. I shall, even out of office, continue to give my modest support to our noble cause of unity, peace, stability and development of our sub-region.

I thank you.

A good number of African leaders also visited or wrote letters in solidarity after I conceded. One of them, President of Benin Republic, Thomas Boni Yayi, who was then the Chairperson of the African Union (AU), visited me and all that transpired was well captured by the Nigerian press.

President Goodluck Jonathan and his Benin Republic counterpart, President Boni Yayi, May 14th 2015, Aso Rock Presidential Villa, Abuja.

President Boni Yayi, while addressing State House correspondents after a closed-door meeting with me, said my administration had been of immense benefit to the sub-region and the continental body. He recalled that I had helped resolve contentious issues in many countries in Africa, leading to restoration of peace and security in such countries. *"Nigeria's decision did help all of us, all the countries of ECOWAS."* President Yayi further said:

> *"President Jonathan played a key leadership role to resolve the problems in Mali, Guinea Bissau; and other places. To us, we cannot forget our brother, President Jonathan."*

He commended me for presiding over a hitch free and successful election and for congratulating my challenger, Muhammadu Buhari, even before the result was announced. He said the action was rare in Africa.

While describing me as a "very great statesman" whose example was worthy of emulation.

He said:
> "I came to congratulate my brother, President Jonathan. He is a very great statesman; he organized the election peacefully in the largest country in sub-Saharan Africa. To us, the election was very transparent and peaceful and coming back, he took a wonderful decision by a great statesman, by calling his challenger to congratulate him, even before the final results was released. Usually, in Africa, it is rare. He gave us a very good example of democracy, not only in our sub-region, not only in Africa but also in the whole world. My brother, we like to congratulate you on behalf of the college of the sub-region............."

While commenting on the challenges Nigeria faced with terrorism, he went on to say:
> "He is really a great statesman. He successfully managed and led Nigeria to fight Boko-Haram. It was not easy. Nigeria is a strong country, being able to set the pace in West Africa. Nigeria is a great country and the president is a great president. Nigeria has been the first economic power in Africa. It is not easy."

When he personally visited to express his gratitude with the peaceful outcome of the 2015 elections, President Alassane Ouattara of Cote d'Ivoire described my decision to quickly concede defeat and avoid bloodshed as a legacy for Nigeria and Africa, and a model to West Africa.

He recalled what happened in his country and how I helped to mobilize the leadership of West Africa and the International community to forcefully remove the then sitting President, Laurent Gbagbo, who refused to vacate after losing the Presidential election. His refusal led to a four-month civil war that killed more than 3,000 persons before he was finally forced out by France and the ECOWAS during my time as the Chairman of the Authority of Heads of State and Government.

I was touched when President Ouattara reminded journalists that even as an Acting President at that time, my love for democracy and peace inspired me to mobilise other West African leaders working with France to remove Gbagbo in order to allow the people's will to prevail.

President Ouattara further said:

> *"I came here on a visit to see my friend and brother and to congratulate the Nigerian people on the conduct of the Presidential election. On May 29, 2015 there is going to be inauguration and hand over to the President-elect, President Buhari. So, I wanted to tell you our appreciation over the leadership we have received from you during these years.*
>
> *"You know that about five years ago, Cote d'Ivoire had elections and I won the election and the former president decided not to leave office. This brought the civil war and 3,000 people were killed. We were put in a hotel for protection by the United Nations for four and a half months. We were there without food because the hotel was guarded by the president's men. It was only after four and a half months of imprisonment in that hotel that finally we were able to leave the hotel; after the former president quit and finally left office for me. I am saying this to stress that what happened in Nigeria is a lesson to all of us. Please accept my admiration.*
>
> *"I think that avoiding violence, avoiding civil war when we have elections in Africa should be our utmost objective. People are more important than power and Mr. President, my good friend, I am not surprised about what you did, and I wanted to congratulate you, congratulate the Nigerian people, and congratulate the President-elect."*

The President of Niger Republic, Alhaji Mahamadou Issoufou, was also on hand. He said ECOWAS leaders will forever remember me for my humility in the conduct of Nigeria's affairs and interventions in the West African sub-region.

The United States' Vice-President Joe Biden commended me when he called me on April 21, 2015. A statement by the US Embassy in Abuja after our hearty conversation reads:

> *"Vice President Joe Biden spoke today with Nigerian President Goodluck Jonathan to commend him for his leadership in ensuring Nigeria's recent elections were peaceful and orderly. The Vice President encouraged President Jonathan to remain engaged and play a leadership role in global issues after his Presidency ends."*

The Presidents of France, Francois Hollande, the President of the USA, Barrack Obama, as well as the Prime Minister of the United Kingdom, David Cameron, also sent congratulatory messages.

These regional and global leaders understand best what was averted. They are very familiar with the consequences of post-election violence and the killings that result from power tussles on the continent. The harsh reality is that there are only a handful of countries in Africa that have not been through the vicious cycle of election related violence. This is why my decision got so much commendation from around the world.

It was quite unique that a President who "lost" an election could receive so many congratulatory messages from home and abroad. The irony is that I received more applause in 2015 than I did after my election victory in 2011.

Chapter Ten

THE CHANGE GAME BEGINS

"In the interest of democracy and development, we must seek to build a nation of strong institutions and systems that serve the poor as well as the rich, the powerless and the powerful in equal measure under God."

Goodluck Ebele Jonathan
*MAY 22, 2010: AT THE FIRST CONVOCATION CEREMONY OF
THE GOMBE STATE UNIVERSITY*

Though we were from different political parties, the major undertaking for me after the election was to demonstrate that our country was far more important than partisan considerations and to ensure there was a smooth transition from my administration to the incoming Buhari administration. My top priority was a peaceful Nigeria.

We needed to relate in the interest of the country to have a peaceful handover in 2015. Former Head of State, General Abdusalami Abubakar, was most supportive. He encouraged both of us to meet on different occasions with the sole intention of putting Nigeria first. By having these meetings, we created a concerted platform before the formal handover.

Unfortunately, what followed after the new government took charge was different. The handover was just a formal ceremony. Our initial meetings centred on moving the country forward. We managed to have some friendly productive talks. As part of the handover programme, the incoming and outgoing governments set up transition teams designed to work together.

Initially, there was a misunderstanding. The incoming team wanted to bring in consultants to work with them. I declined the request, assuring them that when the handover takes place, Permanent Secretaries and Directors would not leave with me since they are civil servants and will be available to brief the staff of the incoming President on all details. I passionately opposed the idea knowing that it would send the wrong message and appear like they were investigating my government while I was still the President.

Incidentally, I found out days later that the request did not come from President-elect Buhari, but rather from overzealous party members. Subsequently, both teams worked together effectively. It took weeks to gather all the data and statistics from the numerous Agencies and Departments of Government.

One may wonder if the transition was difficult for me having been President for five years. It was a mixed bag of feelings. I had no ill feelings because I meant well and wanted to do the best for my country. Yes, there were some human errors along the way as is the case with all humans. I was glad that I handed over peacefuly. My concern was whether the incoming administration would go on a persecution spree of those who supported me or focus on nation building.

Initially, the concern was not necessarily on the incoming President, because having been a Governor and a President, I was very much aware that many unfortunate tendencies and measures come from different camps, especially those with strong connections to the corridors of power.

Sometimes, the intentions of people around you are unclear and they take advantage of certain situations. I tried to have several discussions on this very subject directly with President-elect Buhari in our various meetings.

Two days before handing over the mantle of leadership, I was invited to an elaborate send-forth event that attracted top Nigerians from all walks of life which held in Kpaduma Hills, Asokoro, Abuja. The invitation took me by surprise. I thought that people would run away from someone who just lost an election and here I was being honoured by DAAR Communications Group. I remember feeling most relaxed on the drive out to Kpaduma Hills, knowing that this event was good for me. It would give me another chance to speak directly and appreciate Nigerians for giving me the opportunity to serve.

They lined up several speakers who made my evening. Amongst them were High Chief Raymond Dokpesi, the Chairman of DAAR Communications Group who appreciated my being there. The others were Professor Jerry Gana, Mainassara Illo, Senator Ben Obi and Yinka Odumakin who wished that my late aide, Oronto Douglas was part of the closure. There were also good renditions from Nigerian musicians.

Oronto Douglas, lawyer, popular environmental rights activist and advocate of the Niger Delta, who was my Special Adviser on Research, Documentation and Strategy, had just passed on after years of suffering from cancer. His situation had deteriorated before the elections, and he had almost become incapacitated. Few days after we lost the elections, he died but not before offering me words of encouragement when I visited him. Until his last breath, he was still documenting my legacies and passing out instructions on what they should do in his absence. This became one of the sad events I had to grapple with during the period. At Kpaduma Hills, Oronto's memory had been rekindled by Yinka Odumakin, his fellow pro-democracy campaigner.

I was surprised that the audio recording of the phone call I made to Buhari had been leaked and it was all over the place on the mainstream and social media. Dokpesi and his team played the recorded audio for everybody in the hall. Daar Communications Group gave me more than they will ever know and it helped weave the fabrics necessary for the Transition Hours ahead of me and my future life as a private citizen.

The event of May 27, 2015 drove home the point that the historic day was quickly approaching. An inspection of the facilities of the Presidential Villa was scheduled.

My Vice-President, the President-elect, his Vice-President-elect and I took part in this event. I showed the President-elect sections of the Villa that the President uses, while my Vice President, Arc. Namadi Sambo did the same to the Vice President-elect. Later that day, a small ceremony took place in the Executive Council Chamber where I presented to the then President-elect the handover notes collated by Ministers, Heads of Departments and Agencies of my government.

Muhammadu Buhari was the first to commend me, saying: *"Since that telephone call you made, you have changed the course of Nigeria's political history. For that, you have earned yourself a place in our history for stabilizing the multi-party democratic system. You have earned the respect of not only Nigerians, but also world leaders. You could have made things difficult if you wanted to".*

The handover notes presented consisted of our government philosophy, strategies, policies, programs and activities of my administration for the period between 2011 and 2015. In these notes were also the objectives, targets, tactics, achievements and challenges of our key policies and initiatives, as well as the status of commitments and liabilities of the various Ministries, Departments and Agencies of the Federal Government of Nigeria.

I spoke with conviction about our many achievements. I also mentioned a few major successes like the improved revenue generation, electoral reform, revamping of the rail system, remodelling of our airports, and privatization of the power sector. I handed over the mission statement and commitment of my government for the past five years which I believed would serve as a guide to help navigate the country in the direction it needed to go.

One other document that I gave the President-elect was of utmost importance to me and even more significant than the main handover notes. It was a document compiled by an array of distinguished Nigerians, containing the report of the 2014 National Conference. I was clear in advising that this should not be allowed to end in the dustbin of history as it was very close to the heart of majority of our people and represented our national yearning, going forward.

Let me recap the significance of that document. Four hundred and ninety two Nigerians from all walks of life gathered in Abuja on March 17, 2014 to attend a National Conference that my Government had no influence over in any way other than the fact that I initiated and inaugurated it.

After a very dynamic effort, most of the recommendations and suggestions were based on the need to give our country a working architecture of governance.

The findings resulted in ways our politics could run more efficiently. By the time the conference wrapped up on August 14, 2014, Nigeria was already in the throes of electioneering campaigns for the 2015 General Elections.

Given the limited time we had, my estimation was that the process of implementation could not have been completed in less than one year. This is because I believed that a transparent process of any level of implementation would have involved committee deliberations, public hearings, town hall consultations as well as the endorsement by State and National Assemblies.

Those who say that my administration should have implemented the Confab recommendations forget that I received the report few months before the last general elections and at a time when the National Assembly was on break. Also, this was when the National Assembly was engulfed by so much tension and distrust. The Speaker of the House of Representatives Hon. Aminu Waziri Tambuwal had led some members to defect to the APC, the then main opposition party. The Senate also suffered a number of defections.

At that time, the National Assembly was therefore not conducive for the healthy deliberations and consideration of such an important document. It was obvious that some members of the National Assembly and their collaborators were ready to shoot down anything that in their thinking would improve the image of my government.

To demonstrate my firm belief in the fact that in those 600 recommendations lie a good future for our country, I still ensured that the report was laid before the National Assembly, hoping that some concerned patriots of like mind would see the need to take it to the next level. I emphasized the importance of the conference the day I inaugurated it when I said:

> "The conference is being convened to engage in intense introspection about the political and socio-economic challenges confronting our nation and to chart the best and most acceptable way for the resolution of such challenges in the collective interests of the constituent parts of our fatherland. This coming together under one roof to confer and build a fresh national consensus for the amicable resolution of issues that still cause friction among our people must be an essential part of the process of building a more united, stronger and progressive nation.
>
> We cannot continue to fold our arms and assume that things will straighten themselves out in due course, instead of taking practical steps to overcome impediments on our path to true nationhood, rapid development and national prosperity."

And below is my speech when I accepted the report on August 21, 2014:

> Mr Chairman, very distinguished delegates, it is with all gladness that I address you this day. After nearly five months endeavour to find the appropriate verb for the noun of our country within the syntax of human experience, you have brought to a grateful Nation, the report of the 2014 National Conference.
>
> I want to congratulate the Chairman and his able team, the Delegates, all Nigerians and indeed everyone who has contributed one way or the other to the successful convocation and

conclusion of the Conference.

I also congratulate the Presidential Advisory Committee which developed the framework for the Conference after travelling around the country. We cannot afford to take for granted the efforts and commitment that the delegates and the leaders put into the Conference to make it a success. The patriotic zeal was evident in the inputs of the delegates into the dialogue and how these have now formed the basis of the report.

On behalf of all Nigerians, let me thank you most sincerely for your hard work. Your tireless efforts aimed at coming up with recommendations to chart a path of peaceful coexistence, sustainable development, justice and progress as we march into our second centenary shall not be in vain.

To my mind, one of the main reasons for which the Conference was convoked was fully achieved: that is, to create a platform for a genuine and sincere dialogue among Nigerians. Even in moments when things seemed ready to boil over, it was evident that the Delegates were only disagreeing to agree.

It is now very clear that as Nigerians, we have devised a way of addressing and resolving our differences amicably: we dialogue and dialogue until we agree! This is most heart-warming indeed!

My dear brothers and sisters, I am not unmindful that there were delegates who were in this hall when I inaugurated this conference who today are not part of this closing event as the cold hands of death have snatched them. I pray that Almighty God will grant eternal repose to the souls of our departed patriots and protect all the families they have left behind. They would be proud of what you, their living colleagues, have done to end what we started together.

On the occasion of the 53rd Independence Anniversary of Nigeria last year, I made a promise to set a National Conversation in motion in order to advance the course of nation-

building. The agitation had been there for a while and we could no longer ignore it or delay the process. I was motivated by a genuine desire to make our country a better place where we can build consensus in the evolution of a New Nigeria.

When I was inaugurating the Presidential Advisory Committee in December last year, I made it very clear to the committee that it was a sincere and fundamental undertaking, aimed at realistically examining and genuinely resolving, longstanding impediments to our cohesion and harmonious development as a truly united Nation.

At the inauguration of the National Conference in March, I told you the Delegates our expectations. I did say that I expected participants to patriotically articulate and synthesize our people's thoughts, views and recommendations for a stronger, more united, peaceful and politically stable Nigeria.

I urged the participants to forge the broadest possible national consensus in the process. I also warned that we should not to be under any illusions about the task ahead because we would be confronted with complex and emotive issues.

I am very satisfied that the Delegates navigated these obstacles in a very mature manner. There were those who set out to input ulterior motives to our modest efforts at reshaping and strengthening the foundations of our nationhood to deliver better political cohesion and greater development agenda. The naysayers raised false alarms over some phantom hidden agenda and called to question our sincerity and did everything possible to derail this noble project.

The success of this conference has proved the cynics wrong in many respects. Those who dismissed the entire conference ab initio as a "diversion" have been proved wrong as what you achieved has contrary to their forecast diverted our country only from the wrong road to the right direction.

They said the conference would end in a deadlock as

Nigeria had reached a point where the constituent parts could no longer agree on any issue.

We exploded that myth by suggesting that you should arrive at your decisions by consensus or 75% majority threshold.

That was the first challenge you had at this conference when it appeared you were going to break up. There were suggestions that we should intervene as government to "save" the conference at that dicey moment but I insisted that beyond the inauguration we were not going to intrude into the conference in any manner. We kept our promise.

One of the many reasons for our non-interference is this: we have at the conference, 492 delegates and six conference officials who all in their individual rights are qualified to lead our great country and if they were unable to agree on how to take decisions, we would be in real trouble! Acknowledging the quality and patriotic content of the delegates, I was confident; the right thing would be done.

I understand, there were a few outstanding issues yet. That you did not agree on all issues shows the sincerity of the discourse. Nobody was at the Conference to be politically correct. People spoke passionately and argued strongly in favour of what they genuinely believed in. As a result, there were bound to be strong disagreements.

If everybody agreed on every issue, the debate would not only be lacking in quality and passion, it would also be said to have been stage-managed. What we should worry about now is not that there were disagreements in one or two items, but how to manage these disagreements such that nobody walks away feeling short-changed and bitter. It is a major challenge in nation-building as experienced by the biggest democracies in the world. You managed them well and came out tall, fellow citizens.

I must congratulate you! You not only worked out a compromise but you never had to divide the house to take over 600 resolutions which I understand you passed at this conference. You have indeed built a new architecture of negotiation based on trustful give-and-take that is going to be a permanent reference point in our national life.

There were many other moments of anxiety at the conference with avalanche of headlines about possible "walkouts" and "show-downs". However with your sense of maturity and abiding presence of God who put this country together, what we have today is a walk-in and a show-up!

In my inauguration speech on March 17, 2014, I enjoined you as follows:

"We need a new mind and a new spirit of oneness and national unity. The time has come to stop seeing Nigeria as a country of many groups and regions. We have been divinely brought together under one roof. We must begin to see ourselves as one community. We are joined together by similar hopes and dreams as well as similar problems and challenges. What affects one part of the community affects the other."

I'm greatly delighted that you worked that out in practical terms by your patriotic demonstration of the truism that "though tribe and tongue may differ, in brotherhood we stand".

The result of the conference has shown that we are not enemies, neither are we antagonists, no matter our religion, region, state, and tongue. This Conference has reinforced what I have always believed: that Nigeria is here for our collective good.

Mr Chairman, distinguished delegates, there is a wise saying that if two siblings went to the inner recess to dialogue and they are grinning from ear-to-ear when they are done, truth must have been in short supply in their discussions. However, no matter the bitter truth they shared behind closed doors, holding hands when they emerge and not disowning each other is the hallmark of blood being thicker than water.

This dialogue reflects the current issues in the light of the socio-political evolution of the world. I did say before that we cannot proffer yesterday's solutions to today's Nigeria's problems. The challenges we faced at Independence or even at the beginning of this democratic experience in 1999 are not the same challenges we face today.

The discourse reflected our latest challenges. We shall send the relevant aspects of your recommendations to the Council of State and the National Assembly for incorporation into the Constitution of the Federal Republic of Nigeria. On our part, we shall act on those aspects required of us in the Executive.

Let me reaffirm this: Nobody has a monopoly of knowledge. We who are in government need to feed from the thoughts of those who elected us into power. You have done your patriotic duty, we the elected, must now do ours.

As I receive the report of your painstaking deliberations, let me assure that your work is not going to be a waste of time and resources. We shall do all we can to ensure the implementation of your recommendations which have come out of consensus and not by divisions.

In this regard I appeal to all arms of government and the people of Nigeria to be ready to play the different roles that the volumes of reports you have produced would assign to you. It is my hope that with what you have done, our country is on the right road to getting the job of nation building done.

The report of the National Conference, coming 100 years after the Amalgamation, promises to be a landmark in our history. I have always believed that dialogue is a better way of driving change in the community and I am happy that this dialogue has gone very well. With the far-reaching recommendations touching on several areas of our national life, I am convinced that this will be a major turning point for

Nigeria.

We have gone through many challenges in our first centenary, now is the time to hit the track and take our proper lane for the race of progress. Our moment for national rebirth is here. We have to rekindle hope not only within our country but in the entire African continent where collectively our leadership is acknowledged.

Distinguished ladies and gentlemen, in every governance index, we are making progress. In 2009, our life expectancy was forty seven years; it has now risen to fifty-two. We were spending over a trillion naira importing food four years ago, it is now down to a little over six hundred billion naira and still falling! The size of our economy has grown.

We are improving on our infrastructure and now well on our way to self-sufficiency in energy security. We are focussing on education with a view to banishing illiteracy from our country. We have revived our railways and our airports are undergoing massive repositioning. Our sports men and women are now hungrier for laurels and we are recalibrating our security forces to meet the challenges of newer security threat that was brought to us!

Very distinguished delegates, this administration has made the sanctity of the ballot a cardinal focus. Our successes in polls in different states in recent past have shown we are making substantial progress in the direction of making the polls attractive to all categories of citizens in our land so that our best and brightest would not continue to shun the electoral process. Our goal is that Nigeria must quickly arrive at the point where every vote is not only counted but counts. It is free, fair and credible elections that we crave.

Now is the time that we put behind us all the drawbacks that have inhibited us from fulfilling our manifest destiny and realizing our full potentials. We must steadily arrive at the juncture where strife, conflicts and mistrusts would become distant echoes of our past. We must make every inch of our country a space for joyous habitation. Our country must enter a new season of harmony, prosperity and happiness with justice abiding in every hamlet, community and our country. It is the dawn of a new day in Nigeria and the new nation is at the door accompanied by its great men and women, young and old.

All those who have predicted the disintegration of our country at the end of our first centenary would wish they chose another country when the possibilities of the new vision for Nigeria are actualised. In place of disintegration we shall have integration. In place of bitterness and spilling of blood, we shall have sweetness and healing in our land. Henceforth, our country shall become like running water that approaches a rock, rather than stopping it takes a curve and flows on.

Mr Chairman, we arrived at this point with praise to God and gladness in our hearts. I once again congratulate you and your wonderful team and all of you the distinguished delegates, for the great job that you have done in these five months. I would like to implore you all to continue to make yourselves available for service to the nation as that is the hallmark of every patriot.

We are grateful!

On this note, I hereby accept the report and declare the 2014 National Conference closed to the glory of our Almighty God.

I thank you all."

The chairman of the conference, a former Chief Justice of Nigeria, Hon. Justice Legbo Kutigi, in his speech emphasized clearly that this was a free discussion by Nigerians about the future of Nigeria when he said:

"Let me state here categorically, and with the fear of Almighty Allah in my heart, that not once did you interfere or

> *dictate to us in the course of this conference. The only time we tried to consult the President during the conflict over voting percentages at the very beginning of the conference we were told that the issue was for us to resolve. At no time after that, did you meet with us or speak with us."*

The President-elect took the National Conference report from me and I felt confident of it being used to chart the success of a better Nigeria. Two years after and faced with pressure from Nigerians to implement the conference report, it was widely reported that President Muhammed Buhari said that the conference reports should be consigned to the dustbin of history. The Leadership newspaper of October 4, 2017 quoted the President to have said:

> *"I advised against the issue of National Conference. You would recall that ASUU was on strike then for almost nine months. The teachers in the tertiary institutions were on strike for more than a year, yet that government had about N9 billion to organize that meeting (National Conference) and some (members) were complaining that they hadn't even been paid. I never liked the priority of that government on that particular issue, because it meant that what the National Assembly could have handled was handed to the Conference, while the more important job of keeping our children in schools was abandoned. That is why I haven't even bothered to read it or ask for a briefing on it, and I want it to go into the so-called archives."*

It is instructive to note that we handled the ASUU strike with all the seriousness it deserved. We were able to resolve their grievances and their industrial strike was called off. However, no government in Nigeria has been immune from one major industrial/trade union dispute or the other.

Let me end this chapter with something I had said somewhere else, which articulated my expectations from the then incoming administration: "The best advertisement for good governance is its positive expressions of happiness in the lives of the governed."

Chapter Eleven

THE LAST DAYS

"The progress we seek for our country is in our collective hands. I am confident that with this new spirit of national reawakening and our sense of collective ownership of the Nigerian project, a firm foundation has been laid for participatory governance and progress"

Goodluck Ebele Jonathan
APRIL 19, 2011: ACCEPTANCE SPEECH

As we moved closer to the date for the change of government, the nation was filled with suspense. Members of my cabinet, other political appointees and I were packing our personal effects out of our offices and residences. Many of us were preparing to leave Abuja for our home States to have some rest. Some others were planning to travel out of the country for a vacation. It was a different feeling for members of the then main opposition party who were upbeat in their preparations to take over the government.

Pre- Inauguration Dinner

The official countdown had begun. The State House Conference Centre of the Presidential Villa had been set up for the pre-inauguration dinner taking place in the evening of May 28, 2015. Distinguished guests which included Presidents and Heads of States, former Presidents, members of the diplomatic corps, Ministers, Leaders of Political Parties, captains of industry and other dignitaries had started arriving and dinner celebrations were about to take place. The sound of Nigerian music filled the air as each guest was introduced. The main bowl of the Conference Centre was filled with a feeling of exhilaration. The guests, colour and music all depicted the grandeur that pervaded the venue. Everyone sat eagerly awaiting the commencement of the event.

I was announced with my wife along with President-elect, Muhammadu Buhari and we took our seats. Right on cue, the military band struck up and the National Anthem filled the room. As expected, everyone stood in silence out of respect for the anthem. At that dinner, my farewell address was brief because I had already spoken earlier at length about my government's achievements and my hopes for the new administration. The major formal function I performed was the award and decoration of the National Honour of the Grand Commander of the Order of the Niger (GCON) on the Vice President-elect. This was to enable him bear the title and colours at the inauguration which was to take place the following day.

I was happy to express my gratitude to everyone. After saying my goodbye, next on the agenda was a meeting with my ministers in the tea room of the Executive Council Chambers. There was a bitter-sweet feeling as the people whom I had come to regard as family and friends over the past five years bid me farewell.

The then Minister for Special Duties, Kabiru Tanimu Turaki, SAN (who had become my friend and continues to be a loyal associate to this day), spoke for a few minutes. He eloquently praised my efforts and warmly acknowledged my personae. Then he proposed a toast in my honour which was seconded by the then Minister of Water Resources, Mrs. Sarah Ochekpe.

At just a minute to midnight, we raised our glasses for a toast and at midnight, I dissolved my cabinet.

Presidential Inauguration

The morning of Friday May 29, 2015 began very early. It was the D-Day for the inauguration of the President billed to commence at 10:00 AM. The event expected to be witnessed by no less than twenty world leaders, was being held at Eagle Square, Abuja. The day was certainly going to be interesting and I felt ready for whatever emotion came my way. Today after the oath-taking ceremony, I would finally be going home.

This was an event I had chosen to undertake alone so my wife did not accompany me. Dressed in a black *woko*, my traditional attire and my signature fedora hat, I walked out into the beautiful sunshine and got into my official car.

The members of staff of the Presidential Villa including cleaners, cooks, washer men, security men, and more were gathered outside the Glass House which had become my official residence after I ordered the main residence to be renovated for the incoming President. I bade them farewell and with tearful eyes they waved at me and in unison chorused, 'bye bye Sir'. I entered my car and the convoy moved. I was missing them already. These wre very hard-working Nigerians of diverse tribes and tongues who had served their President well.

Azibaola Robert, my cousin, had come that morning to move my last personal effects to the car alongside Waripamowei Dudafa and some of my immediate security aides. Before I left the State House for Eagle Square, I inspected the last guard of honour mounted by the Brigade of Guards at the inner gate of my residence. It was symbolic because it would be my last inspection of the State House Guard of Honour.

The convoy then proceeded to take the five-minute drive to the venue of the inauguration. During the trip, I reminisced over the last four years and reflected on what was next for me going into the future. As we approached the Eagle Square, I saw a cheering crowd lining the streets. For the ceremony, we had taken the pains to ensure the participation of as many world leaders as possible.

Some of the Heads of State in attendance were Jacob Zuma (South Africa), John Dramani Mahama (Ghana), Alassane Ouattara (Cote d'Ivoire), Paul Kagame (Rwanda), Idriss Derby (Chad), Boni Yayi (Benin Republic), Theodore Nguema (Equatorial Guinea), Robert Mugabe (Zimbabwe), Macky Sall (Senegal), Ernest Bai Koroma (Sierra Leone), Mahammadu Issoufou (Niger), Mohammed Abdelaziz (Sahrawi Arab Democratic Republic), and Joseph Kabila (Congo DRC). Others are Denis Sassou Nguesso (Congo Brazzaville), Michel Kafando (Burkina Faso), Hage Geingob (Namibia), Manuel Pinto da Costa (São Tomé &Principe), Hassan Mohamoud (Somalia), Haile Mariam Desalegn (Ethiopia), James Igga (South Sudan) and Jakaya Kikwete (Tanzania). Others in attendance were the representatives of some Heads of State, the U.S. Secretary of State and many members of the diplomatic community.

My thought reverted to the official swearing in ceremony that I would be participating in very shortly. The convoy came to a stop at Eagle Square and I exited the car. I went to greet a few people and was thereafter ushered up the platform where I was to receive the national salute.

I met a grand setting. The dignitaries and other guests were all present, dressed mainly in traditional clothing. I went right over and stood to overlook the parade ground perpendicular to the commander of the Military Guard that would perform at the ceremony in full ceremonial military uniform. In his right hand was a brass sword held to attention. He was seated on a magnificent white horse with matching colours. It was an impressive sight. The commander officiated the national salute which was dignified and lasted for some few breathless minutes as everyone participated in honour of our nation. The emotions I felt were sincere and not to be forgotten.

Next on the programme, the commander sought my permission for the parade to begin. After giving permission, I went to take my seat next to President-elect Muhammadu Buhari and his wife, Aisha and my Vice President, Arch. Namadi Sambo.

We all watched the impressive synchronized military parade after which I waited for the oath-taking ceremony which was performed by the then Chief Justice of Nigeria, Hon. Justice Mahmud Mohammed. I then witnessed the flag ceremony followed by the 21-gun salute.

After President Buhari had taken his oath of office, it was time for me to leave. I waved at the crowd. To my surprise, I noticed some of the attendees had misty eyes. This struck me because I believe almost all of them were either members of President Buhari's Party, relatives or friends.

I had arrived at Eagle Square as the President, Commander-in-Chief of the Armed Forces of the Federal Republic of Nigeria with the full Presidential convoy. After the ceremony, I ceased to be President. I was now like any other citizen of the Federal Republic of Nigeria, boarding my personal vehicle to be driven to the Abuja International Airport for the final part of the farewell ceremony in honour of an outgoing President.

Abuja International Airport

Pulling into the Abuja International Airport, I was happy to see my wife waiting for me. With her was a joyous throng of supporters, aides, ministers and party members. She did not have to ask, she knew what I had just been through. She touched my hand gently and together we boarded the flight that would take us to Port-Harcourt International Airport.

As part of the inauguration ritual, we would fly the flagship of the official fleet, code named 'Nigeria Air Force 001' or 'Eagle One'. This was significant, as it would be my last official flight.

The trip was also an emotional one for me because I had worked with the pilots and crew for the last five years. We were like a family and they were flying me in an official capacity for the last time. Everyone was full of emotions.

That flight remains one of the most treasured memories of my transition into private life. So much was happening and now I am happy to share with the reader all the experiences of my home coming.

Port Harcourt International Airport

An enormous crowd of friends and supporters from all over the country met us on our arrival at Port Harcourt International Airport. They had come to welcome me warmly as I finished serving our nation as President. My wife and I came down from the aircraft with cheers, greetings and pleasantries. I remember shaking hands with some of the senior dignitaries.

The reception we got in Port Harcourt lifted my spirits and I could not believe that this was happening to an immediate past President who had just handed over power.

Then we made our way to the waiting helicopter that would take us to my home State of Bayelsa where we would commence a well planned homeward journey, travelling in a special convoy, stopping at two different planned events with celebrations along the way.

In no time, we were nearing our destination. Looking outside the window of the helicopter, my wife showed her excitement. We could barely make out the crowd waiting to greet us but as we got closer, she pointed to the splash of colours worn by hundreds of women all anticipating our arrival. Some were in green and yellow, many in orange and white, others in blue and white. They wore matching clothing that signified the groups they belonged to. As we got closer, the women were all dancing excitedly to the music and waving white handkerchiefs ready to welcome us.

Government House, Yenagoa

The Bayelsa State Governor, Hon. Henry Seriake Dickson, had arranged a civic reception in our honour. Seeing my people celebrating and welcoming me home gave me a sense of fulfilment. They were not disappointed that I conceded defeat. Instead, there was a great outpouring of love for me. I had mixed feelings. I was happy on one side but I was also thinking about the course of future development.

We proceeded to touch down and I must admit, excitement was the emotion flowing through me. The helicopter finally came to a stop and we exited onto a red carpet spread out for our arrival. I looked and saw the line of Ministers, Commissioners, Government Officials and Traditional Rulers led by the Governor and his wife waiting in their traditional dress. Each wore a colourful welcome sash, embroidered with the State insignia around their necks. Once the hum of the helicopter ceased, traditional music rang out loudly from the local band of musicians. The ladies danced and waved to my wife, who they lovingly call Mama Peace. It was a wonderful welcome for us and again I was truly overwhelmed.

I had been thinking about what kind of reception I would receive in my home state, Bayelsa. But my concerns quickly vanished after witnessing the outpouring of love and acceptance from my people. For the next few minutes, my wife and I walked on the red carpet that was spread out in our honour. I shook the hands of my Governor and his wife who were on ground to receive us. There were also friends, ministers, government officials, traditional rulers and elders who had also come to receive us.

Civic Reception in Yenagoa

The welcome we received on the streets was spontaneous and we were astonished. As we drove to the reception venue, people marched and danced along the major road leading to the Gabriel Okara Cultural Centre, where once again, the reception was extraordinary.

We walked into this spectacular auditorium that had been specially set up for a concert, and my eyes quickly caught the banner hanging from the middle of the stage. In huge letters alongside my picture, were the following words:

'THE GOVERNMENT OF BAYELSA STATE HEARTILY WELCOMES OUR GREAT LEADER, PRESIDENT GOODLUCK EBELE JONATHAN BACK HOME TO THE GLORY OF ALL LANDS.'

The Gabriel Okara Cultutral Centre, venue of the civic reception in Yenogua, May 29th, 2015.

After enjoying the wonderfully planned entertainment, time soon came for me to address the people. I walked up to the podium. It was a moment of mixed feelings, but seeing the excitement all around me, I felt truly at home and loved among my people, I then presented the following remarks:

> *I thank all of you here today. I also thank my brothers and sisters outside who cannot come in because of the size of the hall. Firstly, let me say that sometimes, after one is exposed to a high office and it is time to go home, there is always that feeling of anxiety. There are always fears of how he would be received by his people. I had the same feeling because in one way or*

another, I knew my people expected more of me politically.

The truth is that I had wanted to come home quietly but the State Governor, Hon. Seriake Dickson, insisted that my return must be a celebration. I am full of emotion and words fail me at a time like this. I don't know what more to say; the only thing I can do is thank all Bayelsans, Ijaw people, people from the South-South, and indeed all Nigerians for giving me this privilege.

During my term as President, at some sober moments, I used to think that probably, if I had stayed back in Bayelsa, I would have been more useful to my people. But I believe that vacating the Governor's seat here gave others the opportunity to emerge. I am happy that, by all accounts, they have done wonderfully well.

I want you all to know that it is my belief that this new administration will work with Nigerians to make better the lives of the people. I am indeed happy that one of the statements President Buhari made was that he doesn't belong to any clique, but rather he belongs to all Nigerians! I congratulate him for that bold statement."

Applause filled the room. I walked off the stage knowing my people understood. I sat down by my wife and we smiled at each other. The display of affection towards us continued with performances by the Bayelsa State Council for Arts and Culture who paraded an array of exceptionally talented professional musicians, singers, dancers, actors and actresses. The performances were spectacular.

The crowd was taken by surprise when the beat of the reverberating drums rang out. Suddenly an athletic, muscular and well-built man with unusually flexible joints, appeared on stage.

He danced to the beat of the music wearing only long yellow trousers and the crowd went wild as he made unusually deft athletic moves. They were held captive as he danced, shook his body at an exceptional speed and gyrated back and forth. He brought the house down as he did the ever-famous Michael Jackson moonwalk to African traditional music up and down the stage.

I want to mention one re-enactment that sent a great message. Apparently, it had been well thought out for my benefit, creatively exhibited through the talented drama using the imagery of a fish. The enormous costume masquerade of a giant fish uniquely appeared on the stage running and turning like a wild person, taunting the audience to the beat of traditional music. The fish played to the crowd but more importantly it wanted them to read the inscription displayed on both sides: 'DO OR DIE POLITICS'. What type of message was this? The crowd began questioning what was going on. What did this mean?

The music complemented the drama and within some minutes another performer came onto the stage. He held a huge cast net and confronted the fish for a few minutes. The music keeping pace, then with a mighty force he flung the net throwing it over the fish and captured it. The fish struggled and struggled to get free but could not. The music struck up as the drama continued and finally, the fish lay motionless, signifying death. The whole drama symbolised the death of Do or Die Politics in Nigeria. The crowd cheered and applauded enthusiastically as the female dancers dragged the fish off the stage.

DEATH OF "DO OR DIE" POLITICS IN NIGERIA

End of do-or-die politics dance drama

Home to Otuoke

From Yenagoa, the convoy took us to my community, Otuoke, for what would be the last reception of this special day. On the way, we passed many communities where various enthusiastic groups had hoisted banners and other decorative emblems to mark my return. Many rolled out drums as the mood of the celebration attained fever pitch.

We walked into the reception ground, Dame Patience Jonathan Square, to another scene that I would always remember. Taking our seats, we listened to various speeches and finally I was called upon to speak. I was immediately ushered out to the excitement of the people. I felt a little tense but hearing the cheers and well wishes relaxed me, I walked up to the podium about to address my people. I was feeling overwhelmed by the show of love at the reception. The cheers from the crowd lifted my spirit. Feeling emotional, I began:

> *"I was born in this small community many years back. The community has grown a little, but of course, it is still a small village by today's standard. I left the community after secondary school and was living in Port Harcourt by the time I started my political career.*
>
> *One thing with all politicians is that we must always maintain and identify with our base, our unit, where our umbilical cords were cut. This is because, after everything, you belong nowhere else but home, and this is my place of birth!"*

I paused looking out over the sea of faces then continued.

> *"Over the years, during all my elections, my wife and I always came back here to vote. Today is quite significant for me. Homecoming is sweet. Since I left this village, I've never actually come back to spend a reasonable amount of time here. I only found myself coming to spend a couple of nights, before going back to my base. But today is different. All I want to say is that I have come home!"*

The crowd responded enthusiastically, so I decided to say a few additional words.

> *"For sixteen years we have made great strides in contributing to societal development, starting from the state and ending up in Abuja. From my wife, and I, we say a big thank you. We belong to this place; we are part of you. We are back!"*

The crowd received my comments with joy, and I was very happy. Walking back to my seat, the music struck up, the entertainers came on stage, and the singers began to sing.

We sat there for close to two hours, being entertained by some of the young and very talented youth we have in my part of the country. I felt proud that my administration had supported the entertainment industry.

Chapter Twelve

THE YOUTH BULGE

"We cannot talk about rebranding the image of Nigeria if the youth are not rebranded, and there is no future for this country if there is no future for the youth"

Goodluck Ebele Jonathan
OCTOBER 8, 2009: WHILE RECEIVING MEMBERS OF
FUTURE NIGERIA PROJECT IN ABUJA

I had been informed that after I conceded to Buhari and in the euphoria of the moment, youth started trekking for Muhammadu Buhari and I. The media and particularly social media had reported that a certain youth, Suleiman Hashimu had started trekking from Lagos to Abuja in celebration of Buhari's victory. This was followed by Oladele John Nihi, who also commenced a trek to my community, Otuoke, from Abuja. Then several others joined both camps, for Buhari and for GEJ. I had thought it was all a joke. I was too preoccupied with the handover activities to religiously follow Nigerian youth on social media at the time, as I have always done. By the time I knew, the trekkers had covered quite some distance and I was concerned about their health and safety.

On the 30th May, 2015, the day after my arrival in the community, I was able to talk with three of these extraordinary young people who had ended their trekking odyssey in Otuoke. We sat down together and they shared the experience of their journey with me. Their experiences is worthy of mention because they are examples of how deep and selfless many young Nigerians think today. I want the world to know about the determination, struggle and commitment that is growing amongst our young people.

Mr. Nihi, who is from Kogi State, told me how his wife, Abimbola Nihi, positively influenced him to actualize his desire to trek in my honour. According to him, she had been watching the news with him one day and spontaneously proclaimed: *"If there is anyone to trek for, it should be President Jonathan who did not allow his ambition to plunge Nigeria into any political crisis!"*

He told me how his wife encouraged him to make the journey by saying something that resonated within him which ultimately helped him make up his mind. She said, *"The peace that you and I enjoy today emerged from Jonathan's acceptance of defeat and by that action he shamed doomsayers and proved those who predicted negativity wrong!"* Her words articulated his thoughts and further jolted his memory to a commitment I made in 2011. He told his wife, *"I remember that after taking office, the President had declared that he would see to it that the country would have free and fair elections and whatever results he would abide by it. Now four years later, he is doing exactly that!"*

The young man was convinced and became determined, not only on making the journey, but also to declare his commitment to my political philosophy, that my political ambition is not worth the blood of any Nigerian. Before starting his trek, he decided to open a twitter account to inform the public of his intention. On May 4, 2015, Oladele enthusiastically started his trekking from the Federal Housing Junction, Lugbe, Abuja.

He arrived at Otuoke on May 23, 2015, nineteen days later covering a distance of about 490 kilometres. The social media buzz had been launched and it took no time for his story to go viral. The mainstream media got on the bandwagon, and word quickly spread across the entire country.

Below are a few of Oladele's tweets announcing his intention and chronicling #TrekForGEJ hashtag.

His actions inspired two young ladies to join him. The first lady, Gloria Nweke made her intentions known the second day. She had driven to where Oladele was (as it was easy to track him with #TrekForGEJ) and after speaking with him, her mind was made up. She was excited and shared her interest with family and friends. Checking in with her Twitter account (@Gloriaspeaks, she bid family and friends goodbye and arranged a ride to join Oladele. Gloria began trekking with Oladele on the third day.

Through social and mainstream media, they were receiving support of food and shelter along the way. News soon reached the second young lady, Ifey Chukuneku. Already convinced, she joined them at Agbor, Delta State on day eleven. These youth belong to the next generation of leaders who instinctively support peace in our continent. I was touched by their story; I asked the young ladies what had motivated them to do such an extraordinary thing. They expressed how much they were encouraged by Oladele's commitment which had stemmed from what I had committed to back in 2011. Each of them wanted to trek to Otuoke, but were afraid to do it on their own, therefore teaming up was the next best thing.

Oladele John NIHI
@OladeleNihi

It can't be more successful than this. Pix with Our DEMOCRATIC HERO & Mama Peace
@Gloria_speaks
@IfeyChukuneku

8:04 PM 29 May 15

Oladele John NIHI
@OladeleNihi

Everything that has beginning must surely have an END. This is the end of #TrekForGEJ bt the PEACE MOVEMENT continues

10:04 AM 01 Jun 15

View Tweet activity

I was also introduced to four young men, Hon. Abdulkadir Usman Mani, (a Councillor from Funtua Local Government Katsina State), the home state of President Buhari, Hon. Yusuf Shuaibu (Councillor from Birnin Gwari Local Government, Kaduna State), Buhari Auwalu from Bauchi State and Sabitu Ikrah Ahmed from Zamfara State who had all trekked from the Northern part of the country to Otuoke. Abdulkadir and Yusuf, who took off from Arewa House in Kaduna, said it took them 37 days of trekking a distance of over 630 kilometres to get to my community, three days before the May 29th handover date. I was pleasantly surprised to see them there.

Some Trekkers from Northern Nigeria, Abdulkadir, Yusuf, Auwalu and Ahmed.

Listening to this next generation recounting their experience of selfless sacrifice, incredible endurance, positive attitude and remarkable determination was enervating. This is not to mention the health challenges they endured like sunburn, sore feet, body pain, fighting the urge to quit (under the scorching hot tropical sun during their long daily trek). I began to think of the challenges my continent still faced. I thanked them and they left but not before assuring me that when they returned home after the spotlight had faded, they would pursue ideas and plans to continue their contribution to peace and unity in Nigeria.

Despite my tight schedule, I have managed to keep track of the progress of these young men and women on their social media pages of their commitment to democracy and peace building. One of them, Ifey Chukuneku, #GEJTrekker, posted an interesting comment on my facebook fan page in response to my May 29, 2018, democracy day message, coinciding with the 3rd year anniversary of my handover.

The following are excerpts of her post:

> *"Just like yesterday, I remember it all. The build up to 2015 general election March 28th, 2015, a day I'll never forget in my life. A day history was made by a great leader, a hero and a democrat, His Excellency, Dr. Goodluck Ebele Azikiwe Jonathan GCFR.*
>
> *And so, it began on that fateful day, the chants of war from the opposition and its supporters should their candidate lose the election, the tension and echoes of fear on the streets and minds of Nigerians. The voices of nay-sayers and predictors of the disintegration of our great country, our mother- land, Nigeria*
>
> *As the results came in and was announced the chants and echoes of war grew louder. The threats to life and spilling of innocent blood of our people (Just as they did when they lost election in 2011) grew even more fear as in every heart and eyes of the people.*
>
> *And we waited and waited, waiting and wondering what*

will happen next. Will there still be a country called Nigeria? Will the opposition bring terror upon the Nation should they lose the election like they promised? Will President Jonathan accept defeat should he lose? How will he stop this war brewing and the spilling of innocent blood of Nigerians by these agents of doom? What next for us etc.... All these questions were in our heart as the results kept trickling in..., one could feel the deep smoke and cloud of tension in the air.

And just when we all thought it was all over, and that there was no way of stopping this huge calamity from befalling us.... Came the call from His Excellency, the President of the Federal Republic of Nigeria, Dr. Goodluck Ebele Azikiwe Jonathan on that highly tensed Monday evening, 30th March 2015. That one magical and heroic phone call that changed everything....

Oh,' my daddy GEJ, from where do I begin my Thank You? Looking back from May 29th, 2015 to where we are now three years after, all I can say is a very big THANK YOU, your Excellency sir, Dr Goodluck Ebele Azikiwe Jonathan, GCFR. Thank you for loving us more than we deserve, for even when we betrayed that love and trust you had for us as citizens and as a nation, you kept on and is still loving us, having our best interest at heart till this very day.

Trek for GEJ in 2015 was everything and even if its three years after, or ten years or twenty years after, if my bones and body can carry me, I will trek to honour your person and legacy repeatedly.

I love you Daddy GEJ!
God bless you...
God bless our mama Peace...
God bless your family
God bless the #GEJTrekkers

God bless the Federal Republic of Nigeria.
Ifey Chukuneku #GEJTrekker.

Young people under the age of thirty-five, make up nearly 65% of Africa's population. They inspire me to do all that I can to advance democracy in Africa and increase access to entrepreneurial opportunities so that our youth can work their way out of poverty. Oladele, Gloria, Ifey, Abdulkadir, Yusuf and others are part of that inspiration for my post Presidential life which is being actualized through my foundation, the Goodluck Jonathan Foundation, (GJF). I am very encouraged that they are part of the youth bulge spreading across Africa.

African youth want jobs and opportunities to work or to be entrepreneurial. Africa needs philanthropists, entrepreneurs and business executives to support the training and development of the teeming youth on the continent. The continent accounts for a large percentage of the youngest population in the world and it keeps growing rapidly, expected to double by 2050.

It is a challenge, but it also represents an enormous potential for economic and social growth when we create opportunities for our youth. I cannot emphasize enough the fact that job creation is a national security and emergency issue. The world will be a better place if our youth feel a sense of ownership of our economies and more so in Africa.

Chapter Thirteen

PRIVATE SECTOR REFORMS
&
AFRICAN RENAISSANCE

"We are gradually reducing the footprints of Government in business activities through privatisation, liberalization and deregulation based on our recognition that the private sector should be the engine of growth in our economy"

Goodluck Ebele Jonathan
MAY 29, 2012: DEMOCRACY DAY SPEECH

African countries are undoubtedly blessed with huge natural resources. Ironically, many less endowed nations are far more prosperous. Switzerland is a good example. The country has little or no natural resources compared to the nations of Africa, but it is today one of the strongest and most stable economies in the world. This is as a result of deliberate, systematic and consistent policies and programmes towards developing the nation's human capital.

The continent's lack of capacity in this regard condemns us to the sad reality of exporting our natural resources, mostly in their raw form, thus transferring jobs and wealth to other countries. The end result is that while the land is fast becoming desolate due to mining of precious metals and hydrocarbons for export to feed industries in other parts of the world, very few new industries are built in Africa.

If the Tony Blair Institute for Global Change Report is anything to go by, the sub-Saharan labour force will be 823 million by 2040. However, the continent is expected to generate only 773 million jobs by then, having a deficit of 50 million jobs. And on August 4, 2015 the Economist Magazine also projected that Africa's population could reach 2.7 billion by 2050. Other predictions state that if this kind of growth continues, the African labour force could be one billion by 2040, making it the largest in the world, when compared to China and India.

How do we then transform this imminently huge labour force from a consumer market to a producer populace such that businesses and enterprises can thrive particularly in Nigeria with the largest share of the population in Africa? This is a ticking time bomb that needs to be handled as an emergency. I knew that as leaders we had to provide strategies that would begin to address these issues in Nigeria considering our impact on the demography of the continent.

I understood clearly that Nigeria needed a rethink of its development options as experience has shown that Governments in Africa are not the best managers of public corporations. Huge amounts of money are always spent to 'turn them around' but their conditions usually degenerate, from national assets of pride to 'white elephant' structures that are liabilities and hardly serve their purpose. So we needed to, among others, deregulate the economy and privatize state controlled but unproductive corporations in favour of private sector profit driven ownership that will ensure effective increase in economic growth that will in turn provide jobs for our increasing population.

We walked our talk in this regard by embarking on the privatization of some public corporations and carrying out reforms in key sectors of the economy.

Typically, I signed the Nigerian Oil and Gas Industry Content Development (NOGICD) Bill 2010 into law less than two months after being sworn in as Acting President to fast-track the development of local technology, industrialisation, employment generation, value addition and overall deepening of the economic growth in Nigeria. The policy is designed to stimulate local production and industrialization by leveraging linkages in the petroleum industry and other sectors of the economy to boost employment and production. And the law also provided a host of requirements designed to ensure workforce development and technology transfer to Nigerians.

The axiom that knowledge is power is very real especially in this era of knowledge based global economy that is driven by technology. This is the reason why, while in office, I encouraged and supported a reading culture among our children in primary and secondary schools. I knew that we had to imbibe the habit of reading in people, particularly our future generation. It was my hope that this culture will help the young people in these age groups expand their mind, enlarge their world and make them more amenable to good ideas that can lead to good ventures.

I launched the 'Bring Back the Book' campaign in Lagos after I became President, on Monday, December 20, 2010. At the event, I was joined by the only Nigerian Nobel Laureate, Professor Wole Soyinka and we both read to the children and eminent personalities present. While I read from Prof Chinua Achebe's book, *Chike and the River*, Professor Soyinka read from his own book, *Ake: The years of childhood*.

This was a personal initiative and I had planned that whenever I left office it would dovetail into whatever post Presidential mission I embark on. I align with Anna Quindlen's thinking when she said: *"Books are the plane, and the train, and the road. They are the destination, and the journey. They are home."*

Nonetheless, I knew our reality in Africa was different when compared to other developed nations. Our children and youth have been constricted and deprived of opportunities that are readily available to other children and youth elsewhere in the world. We had to provide the opportunity to make education more accessible to every child in Nigeria.

Against this backdrop, my administration established 12 conventional Universities; one in each of the twelve States without a Federal University and two Specialized Universities; the Police Academy in Kano State and the Maritime University in Delta State. I also addressed the huge out of school children population by building 165 *Almajiri* schools in the North. I knew that education would make a lot of difference. Nations grow more by what is between the ears of their people than by what is beneath the ground of the country.

To address the issue of widespread unemployment, especially amongst our youth, my administration made job creation a key consideration for all programmes in our economic development vehicle known as the Transformation Agenda. Our emphasis was geared towards empowering Nigeria's youth to become entrepreneurs rather than job seekers, through deliberate initiatives.

After the 2011 elections, we reviewed among others, Nigeria's place in the world of information and communications technology. I realized that it would be a misfortune for us to miss out in the emerging Information and Communications Technology (ICT) revolution just as we lost out in the industrial revolution. I knew that government had to intervene and contribute to the development of an effective ICT sector while encouraging private sector participation. This is to ensure that the Nigeria youth benefits maximally from the huge opportunities avaible in the ICT sector.

To drive the process we established a full Ministry of Communication Technology. Hitherto, communication was just a department under the

Ministry of information that the main focus was to communicate government policies and programmes to the citizenry.

The new Ministry of Communication Technology was created to reposition Nigeria along the lines of evolving developments in information technology and equip our youth with the requisite know-how to take advantage of this fast growing sector.

Within our tenure, we improved broadband penetration and set up two technology incubation centers, known as Information Technology Developers Entrepreneurship Accelerator, iDEA; one in Lagos and another in Calabar. These centers performed well as innovation hubs that supported many start-ups for the development of Nigeria's software economy. Our efforts as a government in pioneering the establishment of these centers encouraged more private sector and state governments' involvement in the sector.

Presently several states and private sector have keyed into the vision and established new hubs and expanded existing ones in our big cities especially Lagos and Abuja. One can say that about 10 states in Nigeria have encouraged such hubs. I was glad to know that Facebook founder, Mark Zuckerberg, during his first visit to Africa in 2016, chose Lagos as his first stop because of the resourcefulness of the Yaba Co-Creation Hub (CC-Hub).

It was my dream that Nigeria and in fact the Nigerian youth, are not left behind in the emerging new frontiers of technological advancement. So we designed the Presidential Special Scholarship Scheme for Innovation and Development (PRESSID), a special post-graduate scholarship programme to encourage our young graduates in highly technical disciplines. The beneficiaries were selected from those who made first class grades in their respective disciplines from various universities.

It was a scheme that selected the best from the best and sent them to top grade universities in the world. The main objective of this program was to train these youth in high level science based programmes that would launch Nigeria into the world of science, engineering and technology. At the launch of this programme I mentioned that Nigeria is beginning to train young people that will take us to the moon. These youth were being prepared to revolutionalize the country's technological advancement in all key sectors including space and nuclear sciences.

Apart from this, I had my mind set on moving Nigeria forward in other areas of technological advancement, one of which is the automotive industry. I had a vision to ensure Nigeria makes its own useable vehicles. The idea was to encourage local entrepreneurs to achieve this through the Nigeria Automotive Industry Council under the Ministry of Industry, Trade & Investment where companies, like Innoson Motors owned by a very determined Nigerian entrepreneur, Innocent Chukwuma, fit in.

In the same vein, another deliberate policy programme to empower our youth and reduce unemployment was the Graduate Internship Scheme (GIS). This scheme was set up by my administration to grant internship placements for young graduates into private companies. The beneficiaries of the programme got internship placements in various private companies to gain work experience that would prepare them for the labour market and government paid them monthly allowances.

I envisioned that this programme will address the issue raised by most private sector employers that our graduates were unemployable because they lacked experience. I was optimistic that this programme will endure to give more youth the opportunity to grow economically. I felt secure about encouraging our youth and I included that commitment in my handover notes to President Buhari.

I am pleased that the Buhari administration has acknowledged that the GIS has been successful in addressing the problem of graduate unemployment in Nigeria. One of the national newspapers, Vanguard, on 5th September, 2016 reported that,

> *"The Federal Government said the Graduate Internship Scheme, GIS, initiated by the administration of former President, Dr. Goodluck Jonathan, was retained by the current administration because of the positive effects it had on solving graduate unemployment across the country. The government said more than 41,000 graduates had benefited from the programme, with over 35,000 already exited and have secured jobs"*

Another noble and successful initiative of my admisitration was the Youth Enterprise with Innovation in Nigeria (YouWIN). It was an innovative business plan competition aimed at job creation by encouraging and supporting aspiring entrepreneurial youth between the ages of 18 and 45 in Nigeria to develop and execute business ideas. I formally launched the scheme on October 11, 2011.

At that event, a young Nigerian woman, Cynthia Umoru, was given the opportunity to speak and she talked about her farming enterprise, the challenges she faced and what the Federal Government could do about it. She talked about her pains with getting credit at cut throat rates. She went bankrupt in 2007 and almost lost her sanity. She revealed how such schemes could help enterprising young people to establish and expand their businesses. She did not mince words when she challenged Nigerian leaders to invest in Nigeria's youth and reap goodness or refuse to invest in her youth and reap wickedness. I was moved when she said that if we as leaders do not help build our youth, they will build Nigeria on their own and will turn their backs on us. Cynthia got a standing ovation from the audience.

She later benefitted from my administration's Nagropreneur programme, identical to the YouWIN but for youth that were exclusively dedicated to the development of the agriculture value chain.

I must add that Cynthia Umoru is a farmer who owns 16 hectares of farmland in Ogun State from where she supplies chicken to *Tantalizers* (a Nigerian eatery) and *Shoprite* (a super market chain). After Cynthia's speech, the Governor of Ogun State, Senator Ibikunle Amosun, who was present at the event, made a pledge to give her the Certificate of Occupancy to her farm land.

Cynthia's case is not in isolation. In fact we cannot talk about inclusive economic growth without placing focus on women and youth. This is because they play a crucial role in sustaining our development. African women represent an important part of our social fabric playing an active role in our agricultural sector, from farming, processing and marketing of our agricultural produce.

On April 12, 2012, at the Presidential Villa, the accomplishments of the first batch of 1,200 YouWIN awardees were celebrated. Then we decided to design the second edition of the YouWIN especially for women to increase the number of women in the programme. The third and fourth editions, in 2013 and 2014 recorded 2,500 and 3,600 youth awardees respectively. I was pleased to see the increasing number of youth that developed their entrepreneurial ideas and businesses through this powerful programme.

An Oxford scholar, while citing David McKenzie, the Senior Economist of the World Bank, described the scheme as the most successful business innovation competition of its kind in the world. According to McKenzie "YouWin even compared favourably with United States fiscal stimulus, proving 44% more efficient than government spending and 130% more efficient than tax cuts."

He added that the scheme was two and half times as efficient as a 2013 management consulting programme in Mexico, four and a half times as efficient as a 2014 wage subsidy programme in Jordan and almost ten times as efficient as a 2011 vocational training program in Turkey."

The entertainment and tourism industry is another area we gave special attention in our quest to promote jobs for youth and open up Nigeria to the world. Nigeria is full of abundant talents who have worked their way up the ladder by sheer hard work and determination. On their own, with their meager resources they created the renowned Nollywood, the third largest movie industry in the world. The music, comedy and creative part of the entertainment industry was not left out in our drive to encourage and create more opportunities for the youth.

We decided to set up special funds for the entertainment industry, to give soft loans and grants to deserving individuals and enterprises to enable them move further up the ladder of success. The case was simple. While the Nigerian youth have strived to create this industry that has become so beneficial to the country, the government needed to do more to harness their talents and encourage them to grow into competitive massive conglomerates.

The entertainment industry began to significantly impact our economy and was captured on our Gross Domestic Product (GDP) for the first time in 2014.

These are a few of the policies and programmes we established during my administration to enhance job and wealth creation, especially for the youth. The momentum we built was a welcome development and a necessary boost which I recommend to other African nations as a means to help the continent expand capacity and youth development and reduce youth unemployment.

At the 2016 Nigeria Economic Summit, it was noted that Nigeria had emerged as Africa's leading economy and investment hotspot for some of the world's largest brands because of the policies and programmes that we implemented between 2010 and 2015. It was my expectation at the time I left office that the trend would be maintained for sustainable economic growth and advancement. It was also my dream that these ideas, schemes and initiatives which my administration and I began will be sustained to give more youth the opportunity to grow economically and contribute to the economy. These programmes, which we implemented effectively contributed to youth development and value addition to the nation's economy.

We must continue to support the prospect for transformation which our youthful population offers. We have gotten into the habit of asking for help, relief, charity, financial assistance, donations, contributions, grants, loans and subsidies in Africa. This dependency syndrome makes Africa appear helpless and incapable of sustainable economic growth and development of the continent. As I have said elsewhere; "Africa must turn its begging bowl to a basket of opportunities."

What will make our continent great is not just trade and investment opportunities or natural resources, but the resilience of the people. Nigeria alone has 198 million people, according to the last estimate released by the National Population Commission. The population of the ECOWAS region is over 300 million and the entire continent close to a billion people.

We must advance an independent and competitive participation in the global economy by promoting and strengthening private sector led growth in more African economies. We must also do more to create the enabling environment that supports the private sector to thrive and become a vehicle for the continent's human development and economic growth.

I am happy that the African private sector is growing stronger, and is progressively engaging in long-term partnership and growth with foreign investors. I was remarkably challenged by the goals achieved and I will devote my time through my Foundation, beyond promoting democracy and peaceful transitions on the continent, to productive engagements that will work with different stakeholders on policies meant to create the right environment to expand small and medium enterprise growth in Africa.

Chapter Fourteen

A STRONG DEMOCRACY

"The strength and staying power of our democracy is dependent on how much we build a political culture of free and fair electoral contests"

Goodluck Ebele Jonathan
JUNE 3, 2009: AT TELL MAGAZINE'S CONFERENCE ON 10 YEARS OF DEMOCRACY

The African continent has lots of challenges. One of them is control of political power which leads to political instability, lack of good governance and stunted development. I believe that if African leaders realize the ephemeral nature of power and that the bitter conflicts, wars and genocides which the continent has witnessed as by-products of power tussles do not justify the ends they serve, then we would have an enabling environment to address our developmental challenges.

That was uppermost in my concession of defeat in a clime where politicians hardly accept unfavourable election results without crying foul. I knew from the history of the internecine struggle for power in Nigeria that we would surely have a crisis. I am happy that my action has inspired similar developments in the West African sub-region.

I handled the election and transition the way I did to maintain peace not just in Nigeria, but also in Africa. My thinking is that it is better to sacrifice power and gain peace and honour than to sacrifice peace and honour and gain the type of power that led Macbeth to the disastrous end he met with in William Shakespeare's renowned play.

The time has come for African nations to begin working towards having truly independent electoral commissions committed to delivering clean elections that increase the confidence of the people on the integrity of the ballot box.

Though Nigeria made significant progress as a result of my administration's electoral reforms, we must continue to build on what we have and ensure that we plug observed gaps in our system. For instance, the implementation of card readers must be properly re-examined to ensure that they are used in all places to obtain a level playing ground for all contestants.

The kind of confusion created in 2015 should not be repeated in 2019 and subsequent elections. It will be too risky if what happened in 2015 is repeated in 2019. Not everyone will have my restraint. Not everyone would play it the Goodluck Jonathan way. Really, no one had ever played it that way before now. The way of peace. It is my sincere hope that the trees we planted will be watered to bear the fruits of electoral freedom for our people.

As I reflect on my homecoming celebrations, I am glad that a large number of people appreciated the depth of my action. Some Nigerians on their own declared me the Hero of Democracy while some others refer to me as The Face of Democracy. The words 'hero' or 'face' are of little significance to me. But thinking deeply, I know that the message of democracy and orderly transfer of power is resonating with our people.

I only hope that successive administrations will sustain our achievements and make the INEC stronger and more independent.

A New Nigeria

I want to contribute my quota to securing a stable government for the people by encouraging a healthy polity. What promotes a healthy economy is a stable political system. The challenge facing both growing and established democracies is to ensure that elections be expressed in a democratic spirit, and backed up by strong institutions that can develop and sustain electoral integrity.

I am fully persuaded that we need free and fair elections. So what can we do to guarantee we achieve this? We must continue to nurture the democratic spirit and as I travel around the continent, I will continue to advocate that each nation state looks at their action plan by identifying and eliminating challenges facing them such as:

- Nation-First Thinking as opposed to Me and My Tribe Against My Nation.
- Making the Office of the President Less Attractive and the Office of the Citizen More Powerful.
- Granting Financial Autonomy to Electoral Commissions And;
- A Strong Independent Ombudsman to Investigate and Punish Incidences of Electoral Crimes.

One problem we have in Africa is the re-election of a sitting President. Can an incumbent President oversee the conduct of credible elections, not minding the outcome? In Nigeria, I had once proposed a single term of seven years to prevent incumbents from running for re-election because I noticed that when the incumbent is contesting to be re-elected, there appears to be more tension in the country. Of course, some critics fought against this idea thinking it was a ploy on my part to elongate my tenure.

Allied to that is the orderly transfer of power from one leader to the next. This issue has created a lot of conflict over the years. Political leaders prefer to stay in power longer than their term because of the fear of what may happen to them as private citizens. This concern is very real, prompting leaders to tamper with the constitution for the purpose of elongating their tenure. A very good example is the case of The Gambia. Yahya Jammeh had initially and graciously conceded after his surprise defeat during the December 1, 2016 Gambian Presidential election.

The final official results gave the opposition candidate Adama Barrow 43.3% of the vote, giving him a slim 3.7% margin of victory over the incumbent Yahya Jammeh who got 39.6%. With such a narrow margin, Yahya could have asked for a recount or in any way disputed the results but he did not, at that time. He conceded.

However, on December 4, 2016, Hamat Bah, the leader of President Adama Barrow's National Reconciliation Party, gave an international press conference to say his party would probe Yahya Jammeh over his alleged crimes against the Gambian people, things began to change and just five days later Jammeh rejected the election results and rescinded his concession thereby sparking a crisis that almost engulfed his nation.

Mr. Jammeh may or may not have been a saint, but casting all the blame for the stalemate that occurred on him is a bit too convenient. If the National Reconciliation Party had been a bit more circumspect, what happened may not have occurred and The Gambia and the rest of West Africa would have been spared the tension.

This is a lesson that ought to be imbibed by all winning candidates, whether or not they are taking over from a rival. No matter how badly you feel about your predecessor, you need to think about the stability of your nation and focus on leadership rather than on settling scores.

While no elections can ever be perfect, not even in the most advanced and stable democracies, at a minimum, people want their elections to be free, fair and credible. My conviction and determination to reshape the electoral process in Africa is critical, and for that reason I urge all African nations to work with fidelity for the greater good of the African continent.

Having been President, I know the toll the cost of electioneering takes on our system. I still recommend having only one tenure of seven years instead of the popular tenure system of two terms of four years. This, in my view, would make leaders work and do the right thing since the fear of losing election as an incumbent President will no longer be there. There is also the need for electoral reforms that simplifies the electoral process and ensures a reduction in the cost of running elections.

My hope is that African leaders must embrace the concept of democracy that delivers purposeful leadership that improves the lives of the people and envision a secure future for their nation.

Before the election, Muhammadu Buhari and I committed to take necessary steps towards a peaceful electoral process by signing an inter-party agreement. We also agreed to respect the outcome of the ballot. This was an important message to reassure the world that good things can come out of Nigeria. Democracy is not just about fulfilling all righteousness by treating the people to the ballot box that you bring out only on Election Day. Democracy boils down to legitimacy and ensuring that the people have the necessary dividends. Elections must offer valid choices.

Hopefully, in the near future our country would have grown democratically to the point where elections would be based on the programmes and policies of parties and character of the candidates, rather than ethnicity or religious preferences.

Over time, through my Foundation, I will speak to thousands and perhaps millions of my fellow Africans to share my story, my heart and my recommendations on having free, fair and credible elections. In my home country, I am associated with the mantra *one man one vote, one woman one vote, one youth one vote.*

I crave the support of one and all to take my work forward as I have made a covenant to dedicate the rest of my life to the cause of peace, democracy, stability, and good governance - God helping me.

Since issues bordering on democracy are being discussed, it is appropriate to cite a letter President Shehu Shagari wrote to me on my birthday. The letter dated November 20, 2015 which he entitled 'You are a Rare Breed,' reads thus:

> *Your birthday deserves to be celebrated both at home and abroad given your selfless services to our beloved fatherland. Your spectacular commitment in the development of our cherished values of democracy in Nigeria and Africa is legendary. On the African political landscape, you are, indeed a rare breed. Your name shall always be written in gold whenever the history of Nigeria is dispassionately studied and analysed. I watched with keen interest when a few days ago, my friend, the former US President, Mr. Jimmy Carter, showered praises on your Excellency. Your incredible achievements have done pride to both Nigeria and Africa. Mr. Jimmy Carter's abiding love and faith in our country Nigeria, Africa, and humanity in general, is not in doubt. He was the first US President to visit our beloved nation. I had the privilege of visiting him in the White House when I was President of our country.*
>
> *This equally credible testimony from such a global political figure has done lasting honour of you, our nation and Africa. It has endeared you to all and has also assured your deserved place in the annals of nations. Your name shall always be written in gold whenever the history of Nigeria is being dispassionately studied or analyzed.*
>
> *Please accept, Your Excellency, the assurances of my highest brotherly considerations, my prayers, and my very best wishes at all times.*

In a similar vein, Colonel Abubakar Dangiwa Umar (rtd), former Military Governor of Kaduna State on April 13, 2015 released a statement with the title, 'You will Forever Remain my Friend'.

The full statement reads:

> *A famous political scientist once warned that "the career of a politician is too uncertain to make any firm commitment to him". Although, I find this warning immoral and distasteful, it*

truly represents the attitude and behavioural pattern of most of the so-called friends and loyalists of men in power. Most are mere fair weather friends. Come 29th May, 2015 President Goodluck Jonathan will hand over power to the winner of the 28th March 2015 Presidential Election Gen Muhammadu Buhari.

With this seeming loss of political power, he will also lose a large retinue of friends and loyalists; people who would swear by his name a couple of weeks ago. The President like most of his predecessors will suffer the pain of betrayal. I however assure him that there are still genuine friends who will be by him through life's challenges out of power. Mr. President should count on me Col. Abubakar Dangiwa Umar as a steadfast friend. I will continue to maintain an abiding and unalloyed loyalty as a friend and brother. I also wish to advise him to ignore the treacherous actions of those opportunists who are decamping from his party, the PDP to APC at this late hour.

These are people who will not hesitate to renounce God in their pursuit of ephemeral worldly power. They are worthless and a great embarrassment to decent people and bad role models to future generations. Let me use this opportunity to dispel the wicked rumour that my closeness with President Jonathan has always been on account of some material favours he extended to me. Nothing can be further from the truth. I swear and affirm that I have never directly or indirectly, been awarded an oil or non-oil contract by President Jonathan or his Government, as evidence will prove later. What I received and cherish above all is tremendous respect from the President. I intend to expatiate on this in due course.

Let me also express my respect and admiration for President Jonathan's nationalistic and altruistic decision to concede and congratulate the winner even before the final results

> *were officially announced. Mr. President behaved like the Statesman I have always known him to be, thereby, saving the country assured implosion had he behaved otherwise. Mr. President has really made us proud. May the Lord continue to protect, bless and guide him and his family.*

On May 10, 2018, I received a rather heartening letter from retired Major General John W.T. Gbor Ph.D of Patriots Transformation Institute. Coming three years after I left office, I will say that the letter and its contents lifted my spirit and I will like to share excerpts from it, as reproduced below:

> *My support for your bid for Nigerian leadership began earnestly when you were the Vice President to President Musa Yar'Adua. When the President was sick and his condition deteriorated and it became clear that he would be no more, there were moves to hand over power to a Northerner. I opposed it vehemently in defence of the Constitution of Nigeria and the integrity and honour of our beloved country, Nigeria. When the matter became prolonged, I held a Press Conference in Aguda Hotel during which I informed Nigerians of the dangers of not handing over power to you.*
>
> *Those who wanted to smuggle power from you considered an interim arrangement through which they could substitute for another person. I felt this was unfair, not only on your person as the Vice President but also, it was unfair for Nigeria, and it was unfair for all minority ethnic populations in the country. I also told Nigerians that they were risking military intervention, taking a cue from previous developments in the political history of Nigeria. Shortly after my Press Conference, you were officially sworn in as the President of the Federal Republic of Nigeria. I felt highly relieved, not only that the right thing was done but also because of the badly needed political stability for our dear nation…*
>
> *Although you did not win the election, the actions you*

demonstrated to your brought out the intrinsic quality or your personality. This is the leadership quality which I saw in you and which motivated my support for your Presidential bid.

By willingly congratulating your opponent, now President Muhammadu Buhari, and voluntarily conceding power to him, you actually shocked the world. At the same time, your action brought the entire African continent to an unprecedented and unexpected level of political maturity. Your level of political maturity spanned beyond Nigeria to lighten the whole of Africa. The entire continent of Africa came of age overnight. You did Nigeria proud! You did Africa proud! You did the black world proud! And above you brought honor and glory to the Almighty God who is the overall ruler of all kingdoms and nations. Your future is in His hands. God is the God of love and God of Peace. You honoured God and He too will honour you.

Since you left office, you have continued to demonstrate your love for Nigeria. You have consistently worked towards maintaining the peace and unity of Nigeria. The oneness of Nigerians has remained your priority. You have earned my respect and that of all Nigerians who sincerely want to see this nation transformed for the wellbeing of all citizens, and as a united and an indivisible entity.

I have written this letter to express my appreciation of the leadership you provided for our dear nation. Yours was the leadership that accommodated all Nigerians, It was a leadership that conscientiously worked for the peace and security of all. It was the leadership that gave people the hope that Nigeria would become a world power in the nearest future. It was a leadership that gave Nigerians hope for ECONOMIC prosperity and a raised standard of living for the generality of the citizens.

Although you are no longer the President of Nigeria, you remain the President in the people's heart. You were peaceful, you were friendly, and you were nice. You are loved and admired by the generality of the citizens.

I write this letter to re-affirm my confidence in your leadership and your person. You are a great Nigerian and I would like to identify with you.

I received so many other correspondences in my transition hours and a number of them made a great impression on me. There was a handwritten note from a school girl, Miss. Evbarehe Abohengbo, from Benin, Edo State, Nigeria, which I reproduce below:

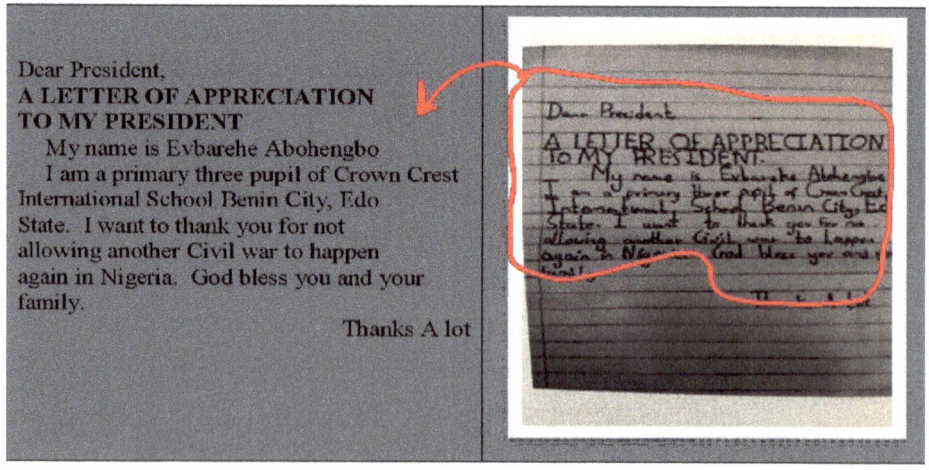

Dear President,
A LETTER OF APPRECIATION TO MY PRESIDENT
My name is Evbarehe Abohengbo
I am a primary three pupil of Crown Crest International School Benin City, Edo State. I want to thank you for not allowing another Civil war to happen again in Nigeria. God bless you and your family.

Thanks A lot

I remember receiving letters from many Nigerian students, including a heart-warming one from Mr. Victor Ogbamgba, from Eluama-Isikwuato in Abia State. There was yet another one which I consider most stirring from a Nigerian student from Delta State.

This particular young man was a beneficiary of one of our astounding scholarship programmes in the country and he wanted to express his gratitude to me for my commitment to building a stable, prosperous, and united Nigeria. He made mention of the political attacks throughout my tenure and went on to thank me for never wavering in spite of how vicious and hurtful the attacks had been. His words were inspiring.

Chapter Fifteen

POST PRESIDENTIAL EXPERIENCE

"African renaissance remains an unfinished business, but the work that remains should not stop us from focusing on new priorities and challenges"

Goodluck Ebele Jonathan
AUGUST 1, 2011: AT A RETREAT TO REVIEW THE NATION'S
FOREIGN POLICY IN ABUJA

The dust of handing over to my successor had barely settled when the political smear campaigns began against members of my family, former appointees and aides. The goal was to destroy everything we did and consign our legacy to the bin. The attacks were so intense that Bishop Matthew Hassan Kukah asked the government and the ruling party to spare some thoughts for my graciousness in conceding defeat without taking the country through bloodshed as we had witnessed before in many African countries.

I remember that after Bishop Kukah and members of the Peace Committee met with President Buhari, propagandists had gone to town with the fable that I had sent the National Peace Committee to the President to plead on my behalf. Let me categorically state that such stories are false. Why would I need anyone to plead on my behalf? What wrong have I committed that I cannot speak to President Buhari myself? I have a conscience that is devoid of bitterness towards any man.

Specifically, to those who accused me of sending Bishop Kukah to plead on my behalf in respect of corruption, I have the following response. The premier global agency universally recognised to gauge corruption perception index stated that the last time Nigeria made progress was in 2014 while I was President. The country had moved eight places forward from 144 to 136.

In any case, after the meeting the peace committee had with President Buhari, Bishop Kukah had this to say:

> *"There is no such thing as probe in a democratic setting like ours. What obtains is investigation, and once people lead and things are not right, investigation becomes necessary. However, in doing that, we must never be distracted from the spectacular actions undertaken by former President Jonathan. He is an individual. I think this whole thing about probe can be ascertained once investigations are concluded. We are saying that a lot of talk and speculation about this probe are the distractions nobody needs."*

Bishop Kukah went further:

> "So, the most important thing is that we need a stable country first, before we can talk about these things, and they would have happened down the line".

In the days and months following my hand over to the new government, I have taken time to adjust to private life while enjoying the certain level of freedom that comes with it. I have also been privileged to travel on some international missions and speaking engagements. I am always humbled when on each stop on those assignments I am commended for the actions I took in office.

In faraway Tanzania, it was an ecstatic moment when the Commonwealth of Nations chose me to lead its Election Observer Mission to the country's Presidential election which held in October, 2015. I walked into the warm embrace of many Tanzanians who were upbeat and confident that my presence would bring credibility to the polls which analysts considered the toughest and closest elections in that country's history.

As they prepared to vote, they were encouraged that high profile observers including myself, who they considered "the Face of Democracy in Africa" and a hero of free and fair election in Africa, would be on ground to observe their elections. They believed that my presence would ensure a free, fair, credible and peaceful election process. Paying tribute to me in an editorial published on the eve of the Tanzania elections, *The Daily News* of Tanzania commended me for promptly accepting defeat in Nigeria's Presidential election of March 2015.

They said, "Jonathan may very well have averted bloodshed that is characteristic of incumbent leaders who cling to power tooth and nail, fang and claw. What lesson is there in this for us in Tanzania, pray."

In the editorial entitled 'Salutary lessons for Tanzania from Nigeria's latest elections', the paper further said: "it is generally admitted, that the election in Nigeria was unprecedentedly free, fair and transparent, whereby the opposition candidate Muhammadu Buhari won the presidency. What is more remarkable is that the incumbent President who sought re-election, Goodluck Jonathan...most graciously accepted the results, promptly."

Finally, they concluded by saying: "I don't know beyond the fact that Tanzania could tragically do worse if it fails to dedicatedly take a leaf out of Nigeria's newest book on elections."

Similarly, the Guardian of Tanzania also poured encomiums on me, describing me as a democrat who pointed the way forward for the rest of Africa. In its own editorial entitled 'High profile figures among observers will add credibility to poll process results', The Guardian stated in its special publication on elections that: *"Jonathan's voluntary handover of power to the opposition wrote a new chapter for Nigeria's democracy, given the fact that it is rare for sitting Presidents in Africa to hand over power to winning opposition parties."*

Thankfully, our presence brought stability to the electoral system in Tanzania.

Below are excerpts from my media encounter after the elections:

Q: How do you feel as chairman of Commonwealth Observer Group, being your first international assignment after handing over, back in Nigeria?"

A: "I am honoured to have chaired the Commonwealth Election Observer Mission (EOM) during such significant elections for the people of the United Republic of Tanzania. Our presence here reaffirms the Commonwealth's support to the country and its democratic process. The Commonwealth Election Observer Mission commends the people of Tanzania for the peaceful and orderly way they exercised their rights to vote on October 25, 2015."

Picture showing His Excellency, Goodluck Jonathan in Tanzania as Head of the Commonwealth Election Observation Mission to the country's October 2015 general elections.

Since then I have led different Election Observer Missions to various nations including Zambia (African Union-2016), Liberia (National Democratic Institute-2017) and Sierra Leone (Electoral Institute for Sustainable Democracy in Africa, EISA-2018). In each case, the sentiment about the positive impact of my presence based on what is perceived as my democratic credentials was the same.

On January 14, 2016, I was given an award by a historic African American institution in the United States for my leadership of Africa's most populous nation, Nigeria, "in human rights, social justice and universal fight for freedom", becoming the first African leader to be so honoured.

The Presidential Award was presented by the Southern Christian Leadership Conference, (SCLC) founded by the late American Civil Rights Activist, Dr. Martin Luther King Jr. I expressed my pleasure at being so honoured. Part of my speech at the event went thus:

"I thank Dr. Charles Steele Jr, President of the Southern

Christian Leadership Conference in Atlanta, Georgia, and the executive of the SCLC for honouring me today. It was a pleasure to meet Naomi King, the sister of the late American Civil Rights leader and founder of the SCLC, Dr. Martin Luther King Jr, who was kind enough to attend the event and identify with the goals and aspirations of the Goodluck Jonathan Foundation. By this award, I am further inspired to continue to work for the advancement of democracy, peace and progress in Nigeria and Africa."

I was thrilled to be in the United States for the 2016 Hope Global Forum Conference, where I addressed the African session as the keynote speaker. The Conference is an annual meeting that gathers leaders from the Fortune 500, including CEOs, private investors, financial leaders and government officials to outline a vision for the modern global economy. The 2015 Conference focused on Reimaging the Global Economy: Inclusive Economies.

On January 27, 2016, I was invited to attend the World Press Conference in Geneva. The press conference was part of activities lined up by the Circle of Diplomats (Circle Diplomatique), Geneva, in my honour and was concluded with a dinner on the same day. According to a statement by Guy Mettan, Executive Director, the Geneva Press Club before the event, I was to address the two crucial topics in Nigeria and West Africa at the press briefing. Mettan said I would talk about Security and Civil Peace in Nigeria and West Africa on one hand, as well as Improvement of Health and Education of Children on the other.

The event lived up to the billing and I presented the following address before a packed audience.

Ladies and Gentlemen of the press, I thank you for coming to hear me speak on the twin issues of education and security. Though this event is billed as a press conference on a Better Security and Education for West Africa, for the sake of time, I will focus on my experience in government which gave me a practical demonstration of how education impacts on security. I will thereafter touch on my post Presidential focus which is on advancing democracy and good governance in Africa and increasing access to opportunity for wealth generation in Africa.

If you peruse the official UNESCO literacy rates by country, what you will find is that all of the top ten most literate nations in the world are at peace, while almost all of the 10 least literate nations in the world are in a state of either outright war or general insecurity.

Lower educations levels are linked to poverty and poverty is one of the chief causative factors of crime whether it is terrorism or militancy or felonies. With this at the back of my mind, I began the practice of giving education the highest sectoral allocation beginning with my very first budget as President in 2011. My policy was to fight insecurity in the immediate term using counter insurgency strategies and the military and for the long term I fought it using education as a tool. As I have always believed, if we do not spend billions educating our youth today, we will spend it fighting insecurity tomorrow. And you do not have to spend on education just because of insecurity. It is also the prudent thing to do.

Nigeria, or any African nation for that matter, can never become wealthy by selling more minerals or raw materials such as oil. Our wealth as a nation is between the ears of our people.

It is no coincidence that the Northeast epicentre of terrorism in Nigeria is also the region with the highest rate of illiteracy and the least developed part of Nigeria. In Nigeria, the Federal Government does not have a responsibility for primary and secondary education, but I could not in good conscience stomach a situation where 52.4% of males in the Northeastern region of Nigeria have no formal Western education. The figure is even worse when you consider the States most affected by the insurgency.

Reports stated that 83.3% of male population in Yobe

State has no formal Western education. In Borno state it is 63.6%. Bearing this in mind is it a coincidence that the Boko Haram insurgency is strongest in these two states? So even though we did not have a responsibility for primary and secondary education going by the way the Nigerian federation works, I felt that where I had ability, I also had the responsibility even if the constitution said it was not my key responsibility. Knowing that terrorism thrives under such conditions my immediate goal was to increase the penetration of Western education in the region while at the same time making sure that the people of the region did not see it as a threat to their age old practices of itinerant Islamic education known as Almajiri.

For the first time in Nigeria's history, the Federal Government which I led set out to build 400 Almajiri schools with specialized curricula that combined Western and Islamic education. I note that 160 of them had been completed before I left office. I am also glad to state that when I emerged as President of Nigeria on May 6th 2010, there were nine states in the Northern part of the country that did not have universities. By the time I left office on the 29th of May, 2015, there was no Nigerian state without a Federal University. Now the dearth of access to formal education over the years created the ideal breeding ground for terror to thrive in parts of Nigeria but there are obviously other dimensions to the issue of insecurity in Nigeria, particularly terrorism.

You may recall that the fall of the Gaddafi regime in August 2011 led to a situation where sophisticated weapons fell into the hands of a number of non-state actors with attendant increase in terrorism and instability in North, West and Central Africa. The administration I headed initiated partnership across West Africa to contain such instability in nations such as Mali, which I personally visited in furtherance of peace. And with those countries contiguous to Nigeria, especially nations around the Lake Chad Basin, we formed a coalition for the purpose of having a common front against terrorists through the revived Multinational Joint Task Force (MNJTF). Those efforts continue till today and have in large part helped decimate the capacity of Boko Haram.

Another aspect of the anti-terror war we waged in Nigeria that has not received enough attention is our effort to improve our intelligence gathering capacity. Prior to my administration, Nigeria's intelligence architecture was designed largely around regime protection, but through much sustained effort we could trace and apprehend the masterminds behind such notorious terror incidences as the Christmas Day bombing of the St. Theresa Catholic Church in Madalla, Niger State. Other suspects were also traced and arrested including those behind the Nyanya and Kuje bombings.

Not only did we apprehend suspects, but we tried and convicted some of them including the ring leader of the Madalla bombing cell, Kabir Sokoto, who is right now serving a prison sentence. But leadership is about the future, I am sure you have not come here to hear me talk about the way backward. You, like everyone else, want to hear about the way forward.

I am no longer in office, and I no longer have executive powers. However, I am more convinced now more than ever about the nexus between education and security. My foundation, the Goodluck Jonathan Foundation, was formed to further democracy, good governance and wealth generation in Africa. Of course, charity begins at home and for the future, what Nigeria needs is to focus on making education priority.

Thankfully, the administration that succeeded mine in its first budget appears to have seen wisdom in continuing the practice of giving education the highest sectoral allocation. This is commendable.

I feel that what people in my position, Statesmen and former leaders ought to be doing is to help build consensus all over Africa, to ensure that certain issues should not be politicized. Education is one of those issues. If African countries could step up their budgetary allocation to the education sector, I am certain that Africa will make geometric progress in meeting her Sustainable Development Goals and improving on every index of the Human Development Index. Data has shown that as spending on education increases, health and wellbeing increases, and incidences of maternal and infant mortality reduce.

In Nigeria for instance, Average Life Expectancy had plateaued in the mid 40s for decades, but after 2011, when we began giving education the highest sectoral allocation, according to the United Nations, Nigeria enjoyed her highest increase in Average Life Expectancy since records were kept. We moved from an Average Life Expectancy of 47 years before 2011 to 54 years by 2015. I had earlier told you about the connection between education and insecurity. I believe that it is the job of former leaders and elder statesmen to convince Executive and Legislative branches across Africa to work together to achieve the UNESCO recommended percentage as a barest minimum. I intend to offer my services, through the Goodluck Jonathan Foundation, for this purpose and I invite interested organizations to help us make this happen.

Ladies and gentlemen of the press, these, in a nutshell are some of my thoughts for a better security and Education for Africa and I will now entertain your questions.

At dinner that evening I was requested to say a few words. This time, I was able to speak of the tensed moments I faced on March 28, 2015 ahead of my decision to concede victory to Muhammadu Buhari after the Presidential election. *"I was actually in that valley on March 28, 2015"*, I told my audience as I narrated why I relinquished power to Buhari, saying I did not want Nigeria to slide into a theatre of war, with my fellow country men and women dying, and many more pouring into other African nations and beyond as refugees.

At the dinner I spoke off the cuff. Below is the text of my speech:

As you can see, I have not come here with a prepared speech, since what I consider appropriate for this occasion is to just thank you all, members and everyone else in attendance, in a few words for the dinner and the award, in order not to make the evening boring. But having said that, I am still tempted to note that if I were to present a written speech, the title, would probably have been "Power Tussle in Africa: A Stumbling Block to Economic Growth." When Mr. Robert Blum, your President, made his very interesting opening remarks, he introduced me as the former President of Nigeria. He was absolutely correct.

However, I believe that not many of you here know that the story of my foray into politics has a peculiar ring to it. I joined politics in 1998 and, barely one year after I got elected as the Deputy Governor of Bayelsa, my state. I later became Governor, Vice President and eventually got elected as the President of my country. I remain the only leader in my country to have travelled that route.

As the President, I served out my first term but, as Mr. Blum had pointed out earlier, I lost the bid to be re-elected. I am encouraged by the fact that many of you here appreciated my decision not to reject or contest my loss at the polls, not even in the courts as many people had expected.

Again, I have to agree with Mr. Blum that it was not an easy decision to take. This is because the allure of power and the worries about what would become of you after leaving office constitute an irresistible force. It has an attraction so controlling and powerful that it takes a man who has the fear of God and who truly loves his people and nation to relinquish power so easily in Africa.

I was actually in that valley on March 28, 2015. I never knew that the human brain had the capacity for such enhanced rapid thinking. One hundred and one thoughts were coursing through my mind every second. My country was at the verge of collapse. The tension in the land was abysmally high and palpable, in the months and days leading to the election. The country became more polarized more than ever before, such that the gap between the North and the South and between Christians and Muslims became quite pronounced.

In fact, it became so disturbing that people began to recall with fear the prediction made some time ago by some interest groups in the United States of America that Nigeria would disintegrate in 2015. And, indeed, many Nigerians did buy into this doomsday prophesy as they began to brace themselves for the worst. As the President, I reminded myself that the Government I led had invested so much effort into building our country. I worked hard with my top officials to encourage Nigerians and non-Nigerians to invest in our country to be able to provide jobs and improve the lives of our people. We worked hard to grow our economy and to improve and bring Nigeria up as the biggest economy in Africa, with a GDP of about half a trillion dollars.

Should I then, for the love of power, watch Nigeria slide into a theatre of war, with my fellow country men and women dying, and many more pouring into other nations in Africa and beyond, as refugees?

Should I hang on to power and tussle with my challengers, while the investments of hard working citizens of the world go down the drain? I then said to myself, NO!

I promised my God that I will not let that fate befall

Nigeria under my watch, hence the historic telephone call I put through to congratulate my challenger, even when the results were still being tallied. I believe that for a country to be great, both the leaders and the led must be prepared to make sacrifices. This is why, everywhere I go, I always advise that the next generation of African leaders must think differently. We can no longer afford to wilfully sacrifice the blood of our citizens on the altar of dangerous partisan politics. It is not worth it. This reminds me of one of my campaign statements to the effect that my ambition was not worth the shedding of the blood of any Nigerian. Some people took it then as mere political slogan, but I knew that I meant it when I said it.

We must all fight for the enthronement of political stability in Africa, for in it lies the panacea for sustainable growth and development. For Africa to record the kind of advancement that will be competitive and beneficial to our citizens, we must have stable states supported by strong institutions. That appears to be the irreducible minimum that is common to all developed societies.

Africa's political odyssey can distinctly be categorised into three eras, and probably another that would later signpost its classification as a developed continent.

Some may doubt this, but it is no fluke that Africa is growing and rising. However I will admit before you here that we still have challenges. That is why people like us did all we could to ensure that Nigeria, the biggest black nation on earth, would not drift into anarchy because such a situation would have spelt doom for the rest of the continent. It would have affected not just Nigeria alone, but the GDP and economy of the entire West Africa. And if the economy of West Africa crashes, it would definitely affect the performance of the economy of the whole of Africa. As you know, the GDP of Africa is less than *three trillion dollars, with only six African countries able to boast of nominal GDP above $100 billion. Even for those in this 'elite' category, you can't really say that they are rich countries. Apart from maybe South Africa that has an industrially competitive economy, the rest are still mainly commodity exporting countries. Even the case of South Africa is not very encouraging, because we have a situation which could be described as a first world economic performance, yet the ordinary people remain poor.*

In the case of Nigeria which is the biggest economy on the continent, the reality is that we have an unenviable per capita GDP of $3,203, which is the World Bank average for a period covering 2011-2015.

Even then, I still believe that Africa has a bright future; a promising prognosis that is supported by the fact that the continent remains a very fertile and attractive territory that yields irresistible returns on investments. I believe that in the next few years many more big investors will be jostling to come to Africa, if only we will do the right thing. The process of getting it right has already started with a democratic and increasingly democratising Africa. But we have to deepen and strengthen our democratic credentials through regular, free and fair elections. This will in turn bring about the stability necessary to improve the infrastructure that promotes rapid economic growth. These are the guarantees that would lead us into the next period which I would like to call the era of a developed Africa. I have no doubt in my mind that we will get there some day.

I will be applying myself diligently to two key areas. First, is to work for good governance by promoting credible and transparent elections. This will bring about the strengthening of our institutions and the enthronement of stability. I also believe that there is the urgent need to create jobs for our teeming young population. This is another area that will be receiving my attention. I recall that the Vice President of your association made reference in his speech to my achievements in that regard through what we called Youth Enterprises with Innovation (YouWin) and the Nagropreneur programme which encouraged young people to go into agriculture.

I believe more programmes like that should be established to promote youth entrepreneurship. That way, we reduce their reliance on paid employment. We will not only teach them to become entrepreneurs, they will also acquire the capacity to employ other people. We will be paying special attention to this segment of our society, especially young people and women. We will develop programmes that will inculcate in them business skills to be able to set up micro, small and medium enterprises. We shall assist them to access take-off grants when they acquire the relevant skills and capacities. There are many areas that they can go into; food processing, light manufacturing and the services sector are just some of them. I can tell you from experience that this works. As we speak, Our Nagropreneur programme, to promote youth involvement in agriculture value chain, is being scaled up by the African Development Bank presently. It is already being replicated in 19 African countries because of the success of the programme in Nigeria.

I invite all of you here today, cabinet ministers, diplomats and private sector people to remain committed to the cause of improving lives, especially those lives in Africa, and making our world a better place. For those of you that will be sharing in this vision for Africa, I assure you that you will not be disappointed. I am very optimistic that if we encourage young men and women in this continent to develop businesses of their own, the story of Africa will change within 10 years.

I thank you all

Again, I was quite pleased when I was invited by the Oxford Union, Oxford University, in October 2016, to present a paper on youth empowerment and entrepreneurship because of its resonance with my well established engagement with youth back home. The programme provided the opportunity for me to reaffrim my belief in African youth and share with the students the experience and outcome of our successful policies and intitiatives that promoted youth entrepreneurship.

Similarly, my keynote address entitled, 'Conscience Based Leadership; the Secret to Global Peace and Security' at a World Peace Summit jointly organised by the State of Sarawak and Junior Chamber International (JCI) in Kuching, Malaysia hit at the core of governance challenges as it relates to leadership recruitment process among youth.

It was indeed a thing of pride to note that the event, which was attended by about 700 young leaders from 102 countries had an enterprising young Nigerian, Pascal Dike, who emerged as JCI's 71st Global president a year earlier, at the helm of affairs.

These and many other international outings have taught me a vital lesson in life: 'no pain, no gain'.

Epilogue

A few anticipated and unexpected incidents have happened since I left office three years ago and the past seems to be repeating itself in some ramifications. For the 16 years that the PDP governed Nigeria, from 1999 to 2015, we instituted purposeful governance and set the stage for meaningful and sustainable development in our country.

Beginning from the Presidency of Chief Olusegun Obasanjo, we stabilized the polity, steered it away from further military incursions and established relevant institutions to set the pace for significant and impactful development. This included setting up institutions to fight the scourge of corruption regardless of party affiliations. We fought to enshrine democratic norms in our society and were determined that the country would not return to any form of dictatorship.

The late President Umaru Musa Yar'Adua, my boss, took over from Obasanjo and undertook to unite the country. He set out to mend fences, placate aggrieved groups and restore peace in the Niger Delta with the Amnesty programme and the creation of the ministry of Niger Delta Affairs. Yar'Adua had a great vision for Nigeria particularly pertaining to the stabilization of the power sector in the country. His was a style of government that was all inclusive. Every region was a key stakeholder. He believed in a government of national unity and walked his talk by offering positions to members of the opposition, although they appeared to have other plans. They did not believe in his government. For them, it was all or nothing.

When I took over from Yar'Adua at the time when he became very ill and later died, the country was facing major security challenges, fueled by insurgency and terror that had gripped the nation. However, by the Grace of God and with the support of many Nigerians, my time in office tackled this scourge and consolidated our democracy. I expanded the frontiers of freedom by ensuring that no Nigerian went on exile and none became a political prisoner in our country. My vision was to build strong institutions and systems that would endure and leave behind a nation with institutions that work for all its citizens. I signed the Freedom of Information bill into Law to enable Nigerians put questions to their government and obtain explanations on the way they are governed. I believed it would help advance the course of freedom, media objectivity and ultimately good governance.

At the UN, Nigeria was elected twice into the Security Council within a period of five years, out of the five times the country had served in the Council since independence. This was unprecedented. I fought insurgency, the worst security challenge in the history of the nation except the civil war. Even with that, we professionally managed and grew our economy to become the largest economy in Africa with a GDP of over $500 billion. All my cabinet ministers, government officials and the private sector worked in synergy to build an economy with well-established strong fundamentals. Nigerians were not under threat by their government. We became the fourth fastest growing economy in the world with an average growth rate of over 6%.

That was the economy we handed over to the Buhari administration. We had something good to offer to Nigerians. We knew what to do to keep our country afloat even in difficult circumstances. In tough and in good times, it was our duty to keep hopes of citizens of Nigeria alive and we were always conscious not to send negative signals against Nigeria and Nigerians to the rest of the world.

As leaders of Nigeria, we travelled far and wide. We marketed our abundant natural and human capacity to foreign investors. We wanted them to invest in the most populous nation in Africa that had within its borders, immense talents, resources and investment opportunities. It paid off because in no time, Nigeria then became number one investment destination in Africa, earning the highest in foreign direct investment. We brought exiled politicians and well meaning Nigerians in the Diaspora back home to be involved in the process of building a greater and better Nigeria. We had a vision for our people. We saw Nigeria in the world stage because we knew we belonged to that stage. Our vision 20:2020 was designed to re-establish strategic development plans to transform our country and set us at par with other economically viable countries by the year 2020. My administration gave the Nigerian women a chance in governance at all levels. We recorded many firsts in terms of women running critical government parastatals.

We initiated the Sovereign Wealth Fund to secure the future of our youth and coming generations. And although it was greeted with stiff opposition by those who later turned around to accuse me of not saving, I am happy it has endured beyond me. My administration created the atmosphere that encouraged our international business partners to grow their respective investments in Nigeria.

I am glad that many of the programmes we implemented have endured the harsh realities that followed my handover of power to the opposition. Under my Presidency, our youth were doing fantastically well in academics, sports and the entertainment industry at home and abroad. Our vision and programmes for our youth fortunately cannot be erased. We initiated impressive youth programmes including the Presidential Special Scholarship Scheme for Innovation and Development, Graduate Internship scheme, Nagropreneur, and YouWIN. We offered grants to budding entrepreneurs and the entertainment industry to enable them create more jobs for our youth.

The youth intervention programmes were designed to produce a youth population that will not be job seekers but job creators, a hopeful demography that would take us to the Nigeria of our dreams.

My determination to reshape the electoral process in Nigeria was a conviction I pursued with vigour. Elections must offer valid choices. Hopefully, in the near future, our country would have deepened democracy to the point where elections would be based on programmes and policies of parties and character of the candidates rather than ethnicity or religious preferences. I hope that politicians would learn that it does not have to be a do or die affair; that others can accept defeat and will play peaceful politics, the Jonathan way. Let our politicians regardless of party affiliations always stand on the side of truth and be able to appreciate the laudable efforts of their leaders. A good example is what Mr. Adams Oshiomhole did on July 15, 2012, even as a Governor from the opposition party. While applauding the conduct of the governorship election in his State, the Governor had said:

> *"I want to appreciate Mr President for his resolve and*
> *public pronouncement that he will provide adequate security for*

> *the people and the INEC staff before, during and after the election. I am glad that Mr. President kept to his words of assurance that there will be no thuggery, hooliganism and violence during the Edo Governorship election. He is indeed a statesman, a man of honour, because there was adequate and effective presence of security agents on ground. I am impressed because the Army actually played a neutral role in the election."*

I recall that the opposition and their sympathisers and campaigners, local and international, with their malicious propaganda, tore our economy to shreds, threatened our stability and existence as a nation and intimidated our citizens, all in the bid to take over power.

Nevertheless, we conducted ourselves in a manner that allowed a peaceful transfer of power from a ruling party to an opposition party, for the first time since independence in 1960. Rather than forge a coalition and build on the momentum we had gathered when they eventually took office, they went on a persecution spree and vengeance mission. That the country slipped into recession soon after we left office was a self-inflicted injury caused by misplaced priorities. The narrative of inheriting empty treasury is a blatant lie. Also, the excuse of the collapse of world crude prices does not hold water.

This is because the Fourth Republic took off in 1999 with crude oil selling for less than $20 per barrel and a GDP growth at 0.58%, according to National Bureau of Statistics figures. Yet the economy maintained a steady growth from that year, peaking at 15.33% in 2002 when the average crude oil price was about $25. It is also instructive that the oil and gas sector constitute about 11% of our GDP. There had to be a wider causative factor than just the fall in world crude prices.

It also amounts to standing facts on their heads to continuously claim that recession was caused by so called mindless looting. The truth is that the opposition, in a bid to undo our government, became its own undoing when it got to power, because of the burden of justifying deliberate misrepresentations.

There is wisdom in the saying that if you win a prize and get the crown, don't go around destroying the person who previously held that prize; it will lose its value. Even after winning the election and forming the government at the centre, the blame game continued. When two brothers fight to death, it is the neighbour that inherits their father's wealth. And we have seen neighbouring nations like the Republic of Benin and Ghana reaping from the capital flight out of Nigeria.

Despite Nigeria's attainment of independence from Britain ahead of most other African countries, we have been increasingly conditioned to seek succour in the blame game. It is time for Nigeria to take responsibility. As Gen. Murtala Mohammed said while addressing the OAU (AU) in 1976 *"Africa has come of age"*. I add that Nigeria has come of age. We either live up to that or we don't. I am convinced that we can, and we should. We must as a nation always strive to improve the quality of life of our citizens and make developmental plans that will focus on the younger generation. That way, Nigeria will not be a liability to the rest of the world. Our population will be an albatross to us and our allies if we do not take the necessary step to turn it into a great opportunity.

The sundry accusations by the new administration would appear to have baited the media. Media trials are entertaining but have little or no effect in fighting corruption and improving the economy. Since I left office, rather than improve on our TI corruption perception record, the situation has worsened with the nation going 12 places backward, becoming number 148 according to the latest CPI ranking for 2017, from 136 in 2014 when I was President. It was bad enough that Boko Haram insurgents continue killing people and ruining businesses but what is worse is when politicians downgrade the economy by demarketing the country internationally.

You should never try to slander your political opponents by destroying your country's economy. Capital flight intensified and companies started laying off staff. In all these, I hope a lesson would be learnt. If you embark on digging a hole for your enemy, you better make it shallow, because you might end up in the hole yourself. How do you attract investors you already repelled through your utterances? Investors are an ultra-sensitive lot. Money runs away from unstable societies.

Most painful have been the attacks on my ministers, aides and associates and even members of my family. There is an attempt to erase our legacy from history. The good thing is that the unending barrage of attacks, deliberate misinformation and programmed media smear campaigns have failed to sway the opinion of those with a clear view of our beliefs, efforts and achievements. There are millions of Nigerians and others around the world who are still impressed with our modest achievements in consolidating democracy and growing the nation's economy. They will continue to serve as my strength and encouragement.

Sometimes I laugh when certain propagandists attempt to stand logic on its head by maligning my administration as one bereft of ideas and 'clueless'.

In assessing my administration, it is best to focus on facts. I cannot assess myself. I leave that to history. But I can assess my cabinet and I make bold to say that never in the history of Nigeria, till date, has the nation had such a star studded cabinet full of achievers and people who got to the top of their chosen fields by merit.

Just consider that my Minister of State for Health, Dr. Muhammed Ali Pate, is now a professor at America's Duke University, as well as a Senior Adviser to the Bill and Melinda Gates Foundation based in Washington DC. My Minister of Agriculture, Dr. Akinwumi Adesina, is now the President of the African Development Bank.

My Co-ordinating Minister, Dr. Mrs. Ngozi Okonjo Iweala, is the chairperson of the Board of the Global Alliance for Vaccines and Immunization (GAVI) and the African Risk Capacity (ARC). She also sits on the board of Twitter and the Asian Infrastructure Investment Bank, just as she is a Senior Adviser at Lazard and a Director at Standard Chartered Plc in the United Kingdom, amongst others.

My Minister of Communication Technology, Dr. Omobola Johnson, is currently Chairperson of Custodian and Allied Insurance Limited as well as the Global Alliance for Affordable Internet.

And it is not just members of my cabinet. Others who served with me in different capacities are also soaring on the world stage. A good example is Ms

Arunma Oteh, who I appointed the Director General of the Securities and Exchange Commission.

Under her steady and skilful direction, Nigeria's equity market grew in geometric proportions, and by the time I left office in 2015 the market had tripled in size to $150 billion in value. Two months after I left office, Ms. Oteh was appointed a Vice President and Treasurer at the World Bank.

These are reputable individuals who served their country meritoriously and who, on the strength of their performance as ministers in my government, are now waxing stronger and valiantly on the world stage with only the sky as their limit.

With such personalities on my cabinet, no one can factually say we were 'clueless' or inept. The evidence of performance is simply overwhelming. We gave Nigeria an impressive and steady Gross Domestic Product growth rate at 6.7% per annum. We were officially cited as the third fastest growing economy in the world by CNN Money in 2014. We eradicated polio and guinea worm and became the first nation in the world to defeat the Ebola Virus, such that the then richest man in the world, Bill Gates celebrated us for our prowess in the health sector. We reduced our food import bill by 36%.

I did the best that I could to preserve Nigeria's unity and ensure a brighter future for all Nigerian children. This remains my driving force even now that I am out of office. I can hold my head high in my post Presidential life to say that under my watch no Nigerian was witch-hunted because of his or her views and not one political assassination occurred under me. The momentum we built was a welcome development and a necessary boost which I recommend to other African nations as a means to help the continent expand capacity and reduce youth unemployment.

These are some of the positive steps I took to guide Nigeria safely to land during the difficult times she found herself. Looking back, I can say that I have a sense of fulfilment. It is said that a good conscience suffers no accusations. I have served Nigeria with all my strength and God alone is the judge of the Universe. I certainly hope that all those who cast aspersions at us can say the same about themselves because the end of a matter is better than its beginning. I had no enemies to fight; I have none still.

It is obvious that the world is happy with President Paul Kagame of Rwanda. The country came out of genocide. President Kagame made propaganda his enemy and got to work. Although Rwanda experienced the worst genocide in Africa's recent history, it is today the toast of the world.

My hope is that African leaders must embrace the concept of democracy that delivers purposeful leadership, improves the lives of the people and envision a secure future for the nation. Africa is critical to global progress and for that reason I urge all African nations to work with fidelity and commitment for the greater good of the continent.

Looking into the future I see that our leaders can do a lot to eliminate ethnic sentiments in our societies, enthrone merit and build a system that gives citizens equal opportunities to excel. A country that cannot use its best brains will lag behind in the comity of nations. African leaders should remove key impediments limiting our growth. When we build capacity in the youth, it will unleash the creativity that would catalyse rapid development.

Since after my handover, and as part of the dedication of the rest of my life to the cause of peace and good governance, God helping me, I have engaged myself in finding ways of advancing the course of democracy and good governance in Nigeria, Africa and the rest of the world, through my Foundation, the Goodluck Jonathan Foundation (GJF). The GJF will partner with all men and organizations of goodwill across the globes who believe in the ideals to which we have committed ourselves. We will seek to prevent conflicts, create conducive environment for businesses to thrive, work to advance the frontiers of education and create employment for the youth as well as encourage them to be self-employed. Millions of our people need help. We need to develop home-grown talents. We must aid educationally disadvantaged children. Nigeria must become the beacon of hope in Africa.

I urge Nigerians and Africans to join me in the effort to create a fresh thinking and enlightenment of the people of this great country and our wonderful continent as we speak out against unrestrained and reckless craving for political office.

We have to rebuild our nations but we must start by rebuilding ourselves.

So let us roll up our sleeves and go to work, actualising our dreams, hopes and aspirations for a prosperous and peaceful Nigeria and Africa.

God Bless my country, Nigeria. God bless Africa.

Annex

United Nations  S/2018/705

Security Council

Distr.: General
27 July 2018

Original: English

Letter dated 16 July 2018 from the Chair of the Security Council Committee pursuant to resolutions 1267 (1999), 1989 (2011) and 2253 (2015) concerning Islamic State in Iraq and the Levant (Da'esh), Al-Qaida and associated individuals, groups, undertakings and entities addressed to the President of the Security Council

43. The predominance in the region of the cash economy, without controls, is conducive to terrorist groups funded by extortion, charitable donations, smuggling, remittances and kidnapping.[69] In Nigeria, 111 schoolgirls from the town of Dapchi were kidnapped on 18 February 2018 and released by ISWAP on 21 March 2018 in exchange for a large ransom payment.[70]

3. East Africa

44. Al-Qaida affiliate Al-Shabaab remains the dominant terrorist group in Somalia.[71] Despite sustained military offensives against it, the group has enhanced its capabilities as it retains its influence and appeal. It has diversified its modus operandi and easily adopts guerrilla warfare when attacked or retreats into the local community for safe haven to reorganize. In late 2017, Al-Shabaab reinforced its presence in Banadir near Mogadishu, enabling it to conduct recent attacks in central Mogadishu.

45. Al-Shabaab mounts attacks mainly within Somalia, targeting the troop bases of the African Union Mission in Somalia (AMISOM), and continues to conduct incursions into neighbouring countries. In early 2018, about 200 Al-Shabaab fighters were killed and others injured, which led to dispersal into smaller groups as a strategy for reorganizing. This disrupted its operations to some extent and had an impact on morale, as some fighters relocated to different parts of Somalia.[72]

46. Al-Shabaab continues to deploy improvised explosive devices as its weapon of choice. Member States assess that the group has the requisite materials and expertise in assembly, that it has enhanced the potency of its improvised explosive devices by increasing the average size in recent years[73] and that it sources weapons and ammunition from local militia and defectors from the Somali National Army and through the smuggling of light weapons from Libya and Yemen (see S/2018/14/Rev.1, para. 39). In late 2017, Al-Shabaab overran four Somali National Army bases and confiscated supplies, vehicles and military equipment of unknown value, which can sustain the group for some time.[74] During the reporting period, the funding sources of Al-Shabaab remained the same (see S/2017/573, para. 47, and S/2018/14/Rev.1, para. 40).

47. Member States assessed that, although ISIL in Somalia is fragile and operationally weak, it still presents a threat because Somalia remains a focus for probable future ISIL operations.[75] ISIL in Somalia has the strategic intent to expand to central and southern Somalia despite its current constraints. Towards this end,

---

[65] Member State information.
[66] Member State information.
[67] Member State information.
[68] Listed as Jama'atu Ahlis Sunna Lidda'Awati Wal-Jihad (QDe.138).
[69] Member State information.
[70] Member State information.

References

Vanguard Newspapers, State of the nation: Have they made Nigeria ungovernable?, May 15, 2013 https://www.vanguardngr.com/2013/05/state-of-the-nation-have-they-made-nigeria-ungovernable/

Okonjo-Iweala, Ngozi Fighting Corruption Is Dangerous: The Story behind the Headlines (The MIT Press), 2018 The MIT Press

International Business Times, Boko Haram: Nigeria President Goodluck Jonathan Should Quit and Convert to Islam, August 6, 2012 https://www.ibtimes.co.uk/Boko-haram-nigeria-president-goodluck-jonathan-resign-370695

Omokri, Reno Facts Versus Fiction: The True Story of the Jonathan Years, Chibok, 2015 and the Conspiracies, 2017 Revmedia

Audu Ogbeh Apologises Over Bringbackourgirls, October 21, 2014 https://www.premiumtimesng.com/news/top-news/169867-apcs-audu-ogbe-apologises-over-bringbackourgirls-gaffe.html

APC warns Jonathan against using Chibok girls as pawns on his political chessboard, Daily Post October 16, 2014 http://dailypost.ng/2014/10/16/apc-warns-jonathan-using-chibok-girls-pawns-political-chessboard/

President Buhari appoints Hadiza Usman as NPA MD, July 12, 2016 https://www.vanguardngr.com/2016/07/president-buhari-appoints-hadiza-usman-npa-md-3-others/

Nigeria president cancels visit to village of abducted girls, May 16, 2014 https://uk.reuters.com/article/uk-nigeria-girls-president/nigeria-president-cancels-visit-to-village-of-abducted-girls-idUKKBN0DW0L920140516

Matthew Kukah diagnoses Buhari, Nigeria, October 4, 2015 https://www.vanguardngr.com/2015/10/matthew-kukah-diagnoses-buhari-nigeria/

Radio broadcast by Major Chukwuma Kaduna Nzeogwu announcing Nigeria's first military coup on Radio Nigeria, Kaduna on January 15, 1966, September 30, 2010 https://www.vanguardngr.com/2010/09/radio-broadcast-by-major-chukwuma-kaduna-nzeogwu--announcing-nigeria's-first-military-coup-on-radio-nigeria-kaduna-on-january-15-1966/

Ihonde, Moses Nigeria: First Call: An Account of the Gowon Years By Moses Ihonde, November 9, 2004 https://allafrica.com/stories/200411090064.html

Omoigui, Nowa, Murtala Ramat Muhammed (1938-1976) https://www.dawodu.com/murtala3.htm

Omoigui, Nowa, Col. Dimka's Failed Coup Attempt http://www.waado.org/NigerDelta/Nigeria_Facts/MilitaryRule/Omoigui/Dimka-1976.html

Take-over Speech by Lt-General Olusegun Obasanjo following the execution of Murtala Mohammed, May 1976, http://www.citizensfornigeria.com/index.php/component/k2/item/576-take-over-speech-by-lt-general-olusegun-obasanjo-following-the-execution-of-murtala-mohammed-may-1976

Shagari's Overthrow Speech by Major-General Sani Abacha, December 1, 1984, http://www.citizensfornigeria.com/index.php/component/k2/item/578-shagari-s-overthrow-speech-by-major-general-sani-abacha-december-1-1984

BBC Hausa, September 15, 2016, Can Buhari get Nigerians to queue again? https://www.bbc.com/news/world-africa-37353145

The Cable, FLASHBACK: The coup speech that overthrew Buhari on August 27, 1985, August 27, 2015 https://www.thecable.ng/flashback-coup-speech-overthrew-buhari-august-27-1985

Nigerian Tribune editorial, 19 years of civilian rule, May 29, 2018, http://www.tribuneonlineng.com/amp/147962/

ChannelsTV, Anti-corruption War: Falana Tasks Prosecution Agencies On Proper

Investigation August 24, 2015 https://www.channelstv.com/2015/08/24/anti-corruption-war-falana-tasks-prosecution-agencies-on-proper-investigation/

PremiumTimes, Elections: U.S. Secretary of State, John Kerry, in Nigeria to meet Buhari, Jonathan, January 25, 2015 https://www.premiumtimesng.com/news/more-news/175562-elections-u-s-secretary-state-john-kerry-nigeria-meet-buhari-jonathan.html

The Nation, Will Nigeria disintegrate in 2015?, December 31, 2014 http://thenationonlineng.net/will-nigeria-disintegrate-2015/

African Business Magazine, Nigeria is top FDI destination in Africa, March 20, 2013 https://africanbusinessmagazine.com/sectors/finance/nigeria-is-top-fdi-destination-in-africa/

Buhari, Muhammadu, 2015 'll be bloody if…- Buhari, May 15, 2012 https://www.vanguardngr.com/2012/05/2015-ll-be-bloody-if-buhari/

Vanguard Newspapers, Post Election Violence: N5m for each slain corps member's family, May 11, 2011 https://www.vanguardngr.com/2011/05/post-election-violence-n5m-for-each-slain-corps-members-family/

INEC, 2015 Nigeria Presidential Election Results, April 2015 http://www.inecnigeria.org/wp-content/uploads/2015/04/summary-of-results.pdf

Vanguard Newspapers, Card Reader reject Jonathan's PVC, March 28, 2015 https://www.vanguardngr.com/2015/03/jonathan-arrives-for-accredition/

ChannelsTV, Orubebe Accuses Jega Of Being Tribalistic, Selective And Partial, March 31, 2015 https://www.channelstv.com/2015/03/31/orubebe-accuses-jega-of-being-tribalistic-selective-and-partial/

Paden, John,
Muhammadu Buhari: The Challenges of Leadership in Nigeria, 2016 Roaring Forties Press

Vanguard Newspapers, Presidential PoLL: ECOWAS leaders hail Jonathan, May 20, 2015 https://www.vanguardngr.com/2015/05/presidential-poll-ecowas-leaders-hail-jonathan/

Peoples Daily, Benin President applauds Jonathan on leadership role in Africa, May 14, 2015 http://www.peoplesdailyng.com/benin-president-applauds-jonathan-on-leadership-role-in-africa/

The Nation Newspapers, Ouattara hails Jonathan for averting 'Gbagbo experience' in Nigeria, April 20, 2015 http://thenationonlineng.net/ouattara-hails-jonathan-for-averting-gbagbo-experience-in-nigeria/

PremiumTimes, U.S. Vice President, Biden, urges Jonathan to remain global leader, April 21, 2015, https://www.premiumtimesng.com/news/top-news/181784-u-s-vice-president-biden-urges-jonathan-to-remain-global-leader.html

PremiumTimes, Remarks by His Excellency, President Goodluck Ebele Jonathan, GCFR On the Occasion of the Submission of the National Conference Report, August, 21, 2014, https://www.premiumtimesng.com/national-conference/remarks-president-jonathan-occasion-submission-2014-national-conference-report/

Vanguard Newspapers, Jonathan's Speech At The Inauguration of National Conference, March 17, 2014, https://www.vanguardngr.com/2014/03/president-jonathans-remarks-inauguration-national-conference/

The Guardian, Historic succession complete as Buhari is sworn in as the president of Nigeria, May 29, 2015 https://www.theguardian.com/world/2015/may/29/historic-succession-complete-buhari-sworn-in-nigerian-president

Vanguard Newspapers, Why we walked 750km for Jonathan Trekkers, June 14, 2015 https://www.vanguardngr.com/2015/06/why-we-walked-750km-for-jonathan-trekkers/

The Economist, March 8, 2014, https://www.economist.com/middle-east-and-africa/2014/03/08/the-dividend-is-delayed

YouTube, Launch of Bring Back the Book, December 20, 2010 https://www.youtube.com/watch?v=w4FULGeze7E

Vanguard Newspapers, 41,000 benefitted from Jonathan's GIS programme FG, September 5, 2016 https://www.vanguardngr.com/2016/09/41000-benefitted-jonathans-gis-programme-fg/

Wikipedia, YouWIN, various dates of publication https://en.m.wikipedia.org/wiki/YouWin!

Vanguard Newspapers, Jonathan splashes N3 billion new grant on Nollywood, March 4, 2013 https://www.vanguardngr.com/2013/03/jonathan-splashes-n3-billion-new-grant-on-nollywood/

Ventures Africa, Nollywood Contributes Massively To Nigeria's GDP, April 7, 2014 http://venturesafrica.com/nollywood-contributes-massively-to-nigerias-gdp/

The Guardian, The Gambia's President Jammeh concedes defeat in election, December 2, 2016 https://www.theguardian.com/world/2016/dec/02/the-gambia-president-jammeh-concede-defeat-in-election

Jollofnews, Gambia 2016: New Leadership Will Probe Jammeh Hamat Bah, December 4, 2016 https://jollofnews.com/2016/12/04/gambia-2016-new-leadership-will-probe-jammeh-hamat-bah/

Daily Post, Stop talking too much about probe, concentrate and do your work Kukah tells Buhari, August 13, 2015, http://dailypost.ng/2015/08/13/stop-talking-too-much-about-probe-concentrate-and-do-your-work-kukah-tells-buhari/

Daily Post, Tanzanians applaud Jonathan as hero of credible election in Africa, October 19, 2015, http://dailypost.ng/2015/10/19/tanzanians-applaud-jonathan-as-hero-of-credible-election-in-africa/

The Cable, Jonathan becomes first African leader to win Martin Luther King human rights award, January 15, 2016 https://www.thecable.ng/jonathan-becomes-first-african-leader-to-win-martin-luther-king-human-rights-award

Africa Development, Africa Health, Human & Social Development Information Service http://www.afri-dev.info/new-scorecard-sheds-light-on-boko-haram-anti-education-stance-52-of-males-in-north-east-nigeria-have-had-no-access-to-education-up-to-83-63-in-yobe-borno-states-alone-nigeria-education-go/

Daily Post, Jonathan replaces Bill Clinton as keynote speaker at U.S event, December 11, 2015 http://dailypost.ng/2015/12/11/jonathan-replaces-bill-clinton-as-keynote-speaker-at-u-s-event/

Ynaija, First Photos: Goodluck Jonathan honoured in Geneva by Circle of Diplomats, January 27, 2016 https://ynaija.com/goodluck-jonathan-geneva-circle-of-diplomats/

Index

A
Abacha, Mohammed 49
Abacha, Sani General 12, 41
Abdelaziz, Mohammed 114
Abiola, MKO 54, 55
Abohengbo, Evbarehe 150
Abubakar, Abdulsalami 12, 49, 53, 96
ABU Zaria, 86
Achebe, Chinua 133
Adesina, Akinwumi 6, 46
Adoke, Bello Mohammed 76
Afeni, Eunice Ayi 6
Africa Development Bank 6, 88, 167
African National Congress, 23
African Union 53, 88, 89
Agwa, Luther Martin 25
Ahmed, IkrahSabitu 127
Alamieyeseigha, Peter Solomon Diepreye 12, 13, 14
Ali, Ahmadu 13
Aliyu, Babangida Muazu 62
All Progressive Congress, 32
AL Qaeda, 15, 32
Anenih, Tony 13
APC, 64
Arewa Consultative Forum, 18
Associated Press, 64
ASUU, 108
Awolowo, Obafemi 48
Auwalu, Buhari 127

B
Babangida, Ibrahim 42, 54
Balewa, Tafa Abubakar 53
Barrow, Adama 144
Bah, Hammat 144

Bayelsa State, 12, 13
Biden, Joe 92
Blum, Robert 163
Boko Haram, 14, 28, 30, 31, 32, 34, 35, 58, 60, 67, 75, 91, 159, 161
Borno State Government, 29
Bozimo, Gordon 12
Buhari, Muhammadu 24, 41, 42, 43, 54, 59, 65, 77, 79, 88, 90, 98, 108, 112, 115, 124, 145, 147, 149
BVN, 146

C
Cameron, David 35, 67, 93
Central Bank of Nigeria, 21
Civil Society, 21
Chambas, Ibn Muhammed 82
Chidoka, Osita 76, 78
Chukwuma, Innocent 136
Chukuneku, Ifey 126, 128
Christian Association of Nigeria, 60
Common Wealth of Nations, 155
Council of State, 67
Court of Appeal, 44

D
Dankwambo, Ibrahim 32
Derby, Idris 114
Desalegn, Mariam Haile 114
Dickson, Seriake Henry 116, 119
Dike, Pascal 168
Dimka, Suka Buka 40
Djibo, Salou 85
Dokpesi, Raymond 97
Douglas, Oronto 97
Dudafa, Waripamowei 113
Duke, Donald 25

Dzzzigau, Emma 23

E
ECOWAS, 82, 83, 84, 85, 91, 92, 139
EFCC, 44
EL Rufai, Nasir 60
Electoral Institute for Sustainable Democracy in Africa, 157
European Union, 88
Executive Council of the Federation, 21

F
Falana, Femi 49
Fawehinmi, Gani 22
F.C.T High Court, 49
Federal Executive Council, 43
Federal Government, 31, 32, 33, 160
Federal Republic of Nigeria, 15, 24, 41, 88, 105, 129, 148
Federal Ministry of Agriculture, 46
Federal University, 160

G
Gabriel Okara Culture Centre, 117, 118
Gaddafi, 160
Gana, Jerry 97
Gbagbo, Laurent 91
Gbor, W.T John 148
Geingob, Hage 114
Goodluck Jonathan Foundation, 130
Gowon, Yakubu 38, 54
Gnassingbe, Essozimma Faure 114
Great Nigerians Peoples Party, 73

H
Hashima, Suleiman 124
His Royal Majesty Ibenanaowei of BassanClan, 12
House of Representatives, 22, 44, 99
Hollande, Francois 35, 93

I
Ibrahim, Waziri 73
ICPC, 44
Igga, James 114
Igoniwari, J. Emmanuel 12,
Illo, Mainassara 97
INEC, 35, 66, 70, 73, 74, 75, 76, 78, 143
Ironsi, Aguiyi 53
Islamic Caliphate, 64
Issoufu, Mahammadu 114
IPPIS, 46, 47
ISIS, 32
Iweala, Okonjo Ngozi 20, 21, 25, 76

J
Jackson, Michael 119
Jammeh, Yahya 144
Jega, Attahiru 75
Jonathan, Ebele Goodluck 3, 11, 16, 19, 27, 49, 64, 83, 93, 129
Jonathan, Patience 12, 121
Junior Chamber International, 168

K
Kabila, Joseph 114
Kagame, Paul 114
Kafando, Michel 114
Kaita, Lawal 15
Keita, Boubacar Ibrahim 114
Kerry, John 65, 67
Kikwete, Jakaya 114
King, Martin Luther 157, 158
Ki-Moon, Ban 82
Kolade, Christopher 25
Koroma, Bai Ernest 114
Kubo, Jonathan 12
Kukah, Hassan Matthew 38, 154

Kutigi, Idris 56
Kutigi, Lebo 108

L
Labour Unions, 21, 22
Laden, Bin Osama 15
Lagos State Government, 22

M
Macbeth 142
Madueke, Allison Diezani 21
Makinde, Ola Sunday 23
Mahama, John 82, 114
Mani, Usman Abdulkadir 114
Mark, David 24
Maritime University Delta State, 134
Mckenzie, David 138
M.D.As, 48
Ministry of Information, 135
Ministry of Trade and Investment, 136
Mohammed, Lai 33
Mohamoud, Hassan 114
Mohammed, Mahmud 115
Msheila, Abba 23
Muhammed, Ramat Murtala 39, 54
Mugabe, Robert 114
Musdapher, Dahiru 45
Murray-Bruce, Ben 25

N
National Assembly, 21, 99, 100, 105
National Population Commission, 52, 139
National Youth Service Corps, 16, 73
Nguesso, Sassou Denis 114
Nguema, Theodore 114
Niger Delta, 14, 15
Northern Elders Political leaders Forum, 4, 14
Nihi, John Oladele 124
Nwankpa, Emeka 23

Nweke, Gloria 126
Nzeogwu, Kaduna 38

O

Obama, Barrack 35, 93
Obama, Michelle 31
Obasanjo, Olusegun 13, 53, 54
Obi, Ben 97
Ochekpe, Sara 113
Odumakin, Yinka 97
Ogbamagba, Victor 151
Ogbeh, Audu 32
Oil Minerals Producing Areas Development Commission, 13
Oshiomole, Adams 22
Okoh, D. Nicholas 23
Okoye, William 23
Olaiya, A.P.J 23
Onwuzurumba, Obioma 23
Opara, Kennedy John
Organization of African Unity, 53
Oritsejafor, Ayo 60
Orubebe, Godsay 75
Ouattara, Alassane 91, 114
Ouedraogo, Desire Kadre 83
Oxford Union, 168
Oxford University, 168
Oyedepo, David 24

P

Presidency, 4, 6, 18, 34, 53
PDP, 4, 5, 12, 13, 15, 16, 33, 49, 53, 59, 61, 62, 63, 78
Pinto Da Costa, Manuel 114

Q

Quindlen, Anna 134

R
Rice, Susan 32, 36
Robert, Azibaola 113

S
Sabo, Ibrahim 30
Sall, Macky 114
Sanusi, LamidoSanusi 21
Sambo, Namadi 15, 116
Security Council of the United Nations, 6
Shagari, Shehu 41, 54, 146
Shakespeare, William 142
Shuiabu, Yusuf 127
Southern Nigeria Peoples Assembly
Steele, Charles 157
Subsidy Reinvestment Empowerment Program, 25
Supreme Court, 49

T
Tambuwal, Aminu Waziri 22, 23, 99
Trump, Donald 5
The Federal Government, 29
The Office of the President of Federal Republic of Nigeria, 6
Transparency International, 48
The United Nigeria Congress Party, 12
Tony Blair Institute for Global Change, 132
TSA, 46
Turaki, TanimuKabiru 113
Turner, A. J. King 12

U
United Nations, 82, 92
United Nations Security Council, 6
United Nations on Trade and Development, 71
United State Government, 49
Umar, Dangiwa Abubakar 146, 147
Umoru, Cynthia 137

UNESCO, 159, 162
US Embassy, 93
Usman, BalaHadiza 34

V
Velocity Capital, 47
Vice Presidency, 13

W
World Bank, 166

X

Y
Yaro, Dogon 42
Yar'dua, Umaru Musa 4, 13, 14, 16, 54, 148
Yayi, BoniThomas 89, 90, 114
Yusuf, Mohammed 14, 15

Z
Zuckerberg, Mark 135
Zuma, Jacob 31, 114

www.ingramcontent.com/pod-product-compliance
Lightning Source LLC
Chambersburg PA
CBHW062214080426
42734CB00010B/1889